The Money Book

June H. Campbell

DALE SEYMOUR PUBLICATIONS

Cover by Rosemary Violante
Photographs by June H. Campbell

Printed in the United States of America.
Published simultaneously in Canada.

ISBN 0-86651-253-5

Order number DS01532

DALE
SEYMOUR
PUBLICATIONS
P.O. BOX 10888
PALO ALTO, CA 94303

Contents

Big Money Mat

About the Author

June Campbell has extensive experience in developing activities for children K-8 and children with special needs. She has Delaware state teacher certification in Art (grades K-12), Elementary Education, and Special Education. She also has Pennsylvania Master's Equivalency teacher certification in Elementary Education and in Special Education for the Physically Handicapped, and California teaching credentials in Elementary Education, Special Education for the Orthopedically Handicapped, Learning Handicapped, and Resource Specialist.

After graduation from the University of Delaware, Ms. Campbell studied at Haystack School of Art, Maine; Viggbyholm Schulen, Sweden; California College of Arts and Crafts, Oakland, California; International School of Art, Venice, Italy; Instituto Allende, University of Guanajuato, San Miguel, Mexico; West Chester State College, Pennsylvania; and the University of California, Santa Cruz, California. She has a masters in Education from San Francisco State University.

Ms. Campbell taught for three years at the John G. Leach School for physically handicapped children, Wilmington, Delaware; for over 10 years at Old Forge School for the physically handicapped, Media, Pennsylvania; and for eight years in Special Education in California. This includes 4 years teaching at Children's Hospital School at Stanford with the Palo Alto Unified School District and currently, Resource Specialist at Grant School with the San Jose Unified School District. Her other teaching experience includes five years as a Home and Supportive Education Teacher for children in Wilmington, Delaware; one year as teacher of art at the Richardson Park School in Wilmington; and nearly one year as a first-grade teacher at the Christiana School, Delaware. She also taught special classroom activities to elementary children in three public schools in Mexico while serving for several months with the American Friends Service Committee. She also served for one year as the acting head of the Occupational Therapy Department of the Governor Bacon Health Center in Delaware.

Introduction

Rationale

The ability to handle money easily and accurately is an essential skill in our society. The activities in this program are designed to help children develop a variety of money skills ranging from simple coin recognition to more complex skills of managing money in a classroom economy.

The program includes facts, activities, and games to help children become thoroughly familiar with United States currency. The classroom economy provides an extended experience that simulates real-life experiences in money management. The system has been used by the author in several classes. The children ranged in age from six to 14, with a variety of abilities and many disabilities. Most classes used the system for one entire school year. One particular classroom used it for five years. Some children were part of this classroom for two or three years. In addition to developing money skills, the classroom economy proved to be an effective behavior management program, one that worked because the children enjoyed it. Also included in this program are many additional activities and games to develop and reinforce money skills through individual or small-group tasks.

Using the Guide

The activities in this guide are divided into four sections: *Introducing Coins and Bills, A Classroom Economy, Supplementary Activities and Games,* and *Big Money Mat.* The activities in the first section should be presented first. Then the classroom economy may be implemented. The activities in the third and fourth sections may be done at any time.

Introducing Coins and Bills

This section contains preliminary activities to help the children learn to recognize and identify the five coins (penny, nickel, dime, quarter, half dollar) and the one-dollar bill. This section also includes many interesting facts about United States currency.

A Classroom Economy

This section describes how to set up a simple classroom economy using facsimile coins and bills that look like real money. The children earn, save, and spend money in a simulation of a real-life economy. The economy may be carried on in a classroom or group situation for an entire school year.

Supplementary Activities and Games

This section includes a variety of tasks, games, art projects, and other activities to supplement the classroom economy or your own ongoing curriculum. Similar types of activities are grouped together, and the activities in each group are arranged in their general order of difficulty. For each activity, the following information is given:

- **Materials Needed:** All the materials needed for the activity are listed in the order in which they are used. Colors, approximate sizes, and quantities are indicated where appropriate.

- **Advance Preparations:** This information is included where appropriate to indicate materials that you or the children will need to prepare *before* beginning the activity. In all cases, *the children themselves* should do the advance preparations if they are capable.

- **Directions:** This is a step-by-step description of how to do the activity. Unless otherwise indicated, *all steps are to be done by the child.* Help the child only as necessary.

- **Individual Educational Objectives:** This describes the skills fostered by the activity and includes specific teaching suggestions for helping a child derive full benefit from the activity. Used in conjunction with the Skills Chart on pages 3-4, this information is helpful in writing individual educational plans for a particular child or group of children.

Big Money Mat

This section includes instructions for making a Big Money Mat and describes a variety of activities using the mat. The activities are appropriate for children at the beginning level of money-skills development.

Skills Chart

The chart on pages 3-4 is provided to help you coordinate the supplementary games and activities in section three with the classroom economy and with your ongoing classroom curriculum. Used in conjunction with the *Individual Educational Objectives* section of each activity, the chart is helpful in writing individual educational plans for a particular child or group of children.

ACTIVITY TITLE AND PAGE NUMBER	gross-motor skills	fine-motor skills	tactile-kinesthetic awareness	eye-hand coordination	motor planning	matching	shape/size discrimination	figure-ground discrimination	parts-to-whole relationships	spatial relationships	sequencing	association	identification	recognition (recall)	number concepts	value discrimination	receptive language	expressive language	written language
	Perceptual-Motor Skills										Cognitive Skills						Language Skills		
	Sensory-Motor Development					Visual Perception													
Coin Cookies (p. 32)		•	•	•	•				•		•	•	•						
Big Coin Rubbings (p. 34)		•	•	•				•	•	•		•	•	•					
Real Coin Rubbings (p. 35)		•	•	•	•		•	•	•	•		•	•	•					
Lincoln and Washington Plates (p. 36)		•	•	•	•				•	•	•	•	•						
Coin Paperweights (p. 38)		•		•		•	•	•				•	•			•			
Coin Tracings (p. 39)		•	•	•	•	•	•	•				•	•			•			
Hidden Money Picture (p. 40)		•		•	•	•	•	•	•						•	•		•	•
Coin Match (p. 41)		•				•	•					•	•				•	•	
Coin Cubes (p. 42)		•											•			•	•		
Coin Feelies (p. 43)			•			•	•						•				•	•	
Penny Rubbings in Patterns (p. 44)		•	•	•	•	•	•								•				
Fingertip Money (p. 45)			•	•								•	•		•	•	•	•	
Money Trays (p. 47)												•	•		•	•			•
Animal Banks (p. 48)				•		•	•	•		•			•	•					•
Put Money in the Bank (p. 49)		•		•				•		•		•	•	•					•
How Much Is a Dime? (p. 50)		•		•	•	•							•	•					•
How Much Is a Quarter? (p. 51)		•		•	•	•							•	•					•
How the Quarter Got Its Name (p. 52)		•		•	•	•			•	•			•	•					•
Floating Target (p. 53)	•			•	•								•		•	•	•	•	
Collect a Bundle (p. 54)												•	•	•	•	•	•	•	
Ball Toss (p. 55)	•				•							•	•	•	•	•	•	•	
Coin Toss (p. 56)	•				•							•	•	•	•	•	•	•	
Egg Box Shake (p. 57)	•		•									•	•	•	•	•	•	•	•
Add It Up (p. 58)													•		•	•			•
Coin-Picture Problems (p. 59)						•							•		•	•			
Egg Box Match (p. 60)													•		•	•			
Fill to Order (p. 61)													•		•	•			
Ten Cents Plus and One Dollar Plus (p. 62)													•		•	•			•
Money Envelopes (p. 63)										•					•	•			•

ACTIVITY TITLE AND PAGE NUMBER	Perceptual-Motor Skills										Cognitive Skills						Language Skills		
	Sensory-Motor Development					Visual Perception													
	gross-motor skills	fine-motor skills	tactile-kinesthetic awareness	eye-hand coordination	motor planning	matching	shape/size discrimination	figure-ground discrimination	parts-to-whole relationships	spatial relationships	sequencing	association	identification	recognition (recall)	number concepts	value discrimination	receptive language	expressive language	written language
Dollar Build-Up (p. 64)									•	•	•	•			•	•			
Money Make-a-Word (p. 65)	•								•		•						•	•	•
Money Word Puzzles (p. 66)		•		•					•	•	•	•	•						•
Money Word Signs (p. 67)		•		•					•		•	•							•
Money Word Mix-Ups (p. 68)									•		•				•	•	•	•	•
Money Sorting (p. 69)		•		•								•				•			•
Money Match-Up (p. 70)											•		•	•	•	•			•
Point to the Coin (p. 71)													•	•	•	•	•	•	
Shopping Lists (p. 72)											•				•	•			
Searching the Ads (p. 73)								•	•		•				•	•			
How Much? (p. 74)								•			•	•			•	•	•	•	
Which Would You Buy? (p. 75)											•	•			•	•	•	•	

4

Introducing the Coins and Bills

Introducing the Coins and Bills

Preliminary Activity

As a preliminary activity, let the children examine all five coins used in United States currency. Give each child a real penny, nickel, dime, quarter, and half dollar, and keep a set of coins yourself, along with a real one-dollar bill to show the group. Have the children count their coins, compare their relative sizes, touch each one and listen as you name the coin and its value, and match each of their coins to one you hold up for them to see.

Have the children arrange their coins in a row from left to right, starting with the half dollar. Arrange your coins in a row on a vertical surface for the children to use as a reference as they arrange their coins. Put a small loop of tape with the sticky side out on the back of each coin, and tape them in a row on the chalkboard or other vertical surface in descending value: half dollar, quarter, dime, nickel, penny. Arranging coins from highest to lowest in value helps the children learn how to count money more easily by adding the highest-value coin first, then the next highest value, and so on.

Naming the Coins and Their Values: To emphasize money vocabulary and language skills, let each child take a turn naming the coins and their values from highest to lowest: "half dollar, fifty cents," "quarter, twenty-five cents," "dime, ten cents," "nickel, five cents," and "penny, one cent." As the child names them, he or she should point to the coins and even pick them up and handle them, feeling the raised surfaces and edges and noting heft and size. This gives visual and tactile-kinesthetic reinforcement in the learning experience.

Comparing Values: Show the children the one-dollar bill, and explain that the coins are worth less or buy less than a dollar. Explain that 50 cents is less than a dollar because a dollar is worth 100 cents, 25 cents is less than 50 cents, 10 cents is less than 25 cents, five cents is less than 10 cents, and one cent is less than five cents. Restate these relationships by saying that a dollar is more than 50 cents, 50 cents is more than 25 cents, 25 cents is more than 10 cents, 10 cents is more than five cents, and five cents is more than one cent. (Use either "buys more" and "buys less" or "is worth more" and "is worth less" in your statements.)

Individual Coins and Bills

After the preliminary activity involving all five coins together, present each coin and the dollar bill in a separate activity. In the following activities, it is suggested that you use both real coins and their facsimiles in order to familiarize the children with the real coins and as an introduction to the exclusive use of the facsimiles in the classroom economy. It is important that each child discover for himself or herself how each facsimile resembles the real coin. (Teaching Resources' *Coins and Bills* may be used for the facsimiles.)

With very young children or children who are at a very beginning level of money-skills development, the coins may be introduced and used in the classroom economy one at a time, beginning with the penny. When the children become familiar with one coin, another may be introduced and incorporated into the economy.

In the following activities, a great deal of information is included about each coin. Decide what is appropriate for your particular group of children and in what order you want to discuss the coins.

Penny

Give each child one real penny and one facsimile penny. You also may want to give each child or group of children a small magnifying glass so the children can examine details on the coins. Call the children's attention to the sizes of the real and facsimile pennies. Have them match the sizes by putting one coin on top of the other. Discuss the color of the coins. Explain that it is the color of the metal copper, and that the real penny is made of copper.

Explain that a penny is worth one cent. Write the words *one cent* and the symbols *1¢* and *$.01* on the chalkboard for all to see. Tell the children that 100 pennies equal one dollar. The children can practice their counting skills as you explain that five pennies equal one nickel, 10 pennies equal one dime, 25 pennies equal one quarter, and 50 pennies equal one half dollar.

Heads

Ask the children to find the side of the penny that has a picture of a man on it. Explain that the man is Abraham Lincoln, who was the sixteenth President of the United States. He became President on March 4, 1861, and served until his assassination on April 14, 1865. Tell the children that this side of the coin is called "heads." In United States coinage, it is called the "obverse" side. (With some children, you may want to call this the "front" of the coin and the other side the "back.") Explain that this side of the coin always bears the date the coin was made or "minted." Have the children find the date and the words IN GOD WE TRUST and LIBERTY. Magnifying glasses are helpful for this.

Tails

Have the children turn their pennies over. Explain that this side is called "tails." On this side of the penny is a picture of the Lincoln Memorial in Washington, D.C., a very popular tourist attraction. Inside is a large marble statue of Abraham Lincoln, and many of his famous sayings are carved on the walls. The Lincoln Memorial is a way of honoring this great man. If any of the children have visited the Memorial, ask them to tell the others about it.

Have the children find the words ONE CENT along the bottom edge of the penny. This, of course, is the value of the coin. The words UNITED STATES OF AMERICA are printed along the top edge. This means that the coin is legal only in the United States and can be used only in this country. Explain that other countries have their own money, and if you visited another country and wanted to buy something, you would have to exchange our money for theirs.

The Latin words E PLURIBUS UNUM are also printed on this side of the penny. The children may need magnifying glasses to see the words clearly. In English the words mean "one out of many," which may be interpreted "We are all one people."

Nickel

Give each child a real and a facsimile nickel. Name the coin and write the name on the chalkboard so the children can see the word as well as hear it and see the coin at the same time. Explain that the nickel is worth five cents, or five pennies. To illustrate this concept, give each child five pennies so he or she can understand the concept visually and tactually.

Have the children compare the real and facsimile nickels, matching their sizes and feeling the raised surfaces on the real nickel. Also have them compare the real and facsimile nickels with real and facsimile pennies, noting likenesses and differences. The two most obvious differences, of course, are size and color. The color of the nickel comes from the metal of which it is made, an alloy of nickel and copper. The metal content gives this coin its name.

Heads

Ask the children to find the "heads" side of the nickel. This side has a picture of Thomas Jefferson, the third President of the United States, who served from 1801 to 1809. Have them find the date the coin was made and the words IN GOD WE TRUST and LIBERTY. Let them use magnifying glasses if necessary.

Tails

Have the children turn the nickel over. On the "tails" side is a picture of Jefferson's home, which he called Monticello. The word is printed below the picture. Monticello is located near Charlottesville, Virginia, and is open to the public. If any children have visited Monticello, ask them to tell the others about it. Also have the children find the words UNITED STATES OF AMERICA and E PLURIBUS UNUM and the value of the coin stated in words, FIVE CENTS.

Dime

Give each child a real and a facsimile dime, nickel, and penny. Have the children compare the real and facsimile dimes. Then have them compare these with the real and facsimile nickels and pennies. The dime is the smallest and thinnest United States coin. The children may wonder why this is so, since the dime is worth more than the nickel and penny. Explain that the dime has silver in it, and silver is a more valuable metal than copper or nickel. Have the children look at and feel the notched edge of the dime. The notches are there to prevent people from filing off some of the silver and then passing the coin as a full-value dime. The same is true of the quarter and half dollar. The U.S. Coinage Act of 1965 reduced the proportion of silver in the dime, quarter, and half dollar.

Heads

On this side of the dime is a picture of Franklin D. Roosevelt, the thirty-second President of the United States, who served from March 4, 1933, until his death on April 12, 1945. The Roosevelt dime was issued on January 30, 1946, Roosevelt's birth date and only nine months after his death. Have the children find the date the coin was made and the words IN GOD WE TRUST and LIBERTY.

Tails

Have the children turn the coin over and find the words ONE DIME. UNITED STATES OF AMERICA and E PLURIBUS UNUM are also printed on the "tails" side. In the center of the picture is a torch symbolizing the light of knowledge and understanding. On the left is an olive branch symbolizing peace. On the right is an oak branch symbolizing strength and independence. You may want to ask the children what these words mean to them.

Quarter

Give each child a real and a facsimile quarter, dime, nickel, and penny. As before, have them first compare the real and facsimile quarters, and then the quarters with the real and facsimile dimes, nickels, and pennies.

Heads

Have the children find the "heads" side of the quarter, and then tell them that the picture shows the first President of the United States. Ask them if they know who it is. It is, of course, George Washington, who served from April 30, 1789, to March 4, 1797. The quarter was issued in 1932 on the two-hundredth anniversary of Washington's birth.

LIBERTY is printed in large letters above Washington's head. IN GOD WE TRUST is printed in small letters on the left. The mint date is at the bottom of the coin.

Tails

Have the children turn the coin over, and ask them if they know what kind of bird is shown. The bald-headed eagle was adopted as the symbol of the United States by an Act of Congress. The meaning of this symbol is that just as the eagle wears no crown, the United States would have no king or queen. Below the eagle is an olive branch symbolizing peace.

At the top are the words UNITED STATES OF AMERICA and E PLURIBUS UNUM. At the bottom are the words QUARTER DOLLAR. Tell the children that the word "quarter" signifies a fourth of something. (With younger children, ask if they hear the word "four" in "fourth.") In this case, it means that four quarters equal one dollar, or four 25's equal 100. When discussing this, show the children four quarters and let them count them.

Commemorative Quarter

In 1976, a special bicentennial quarter was issued with the dates 1776-1976. A drummer wearing the tricornered hat and costume of the early American colonist appears on the reverse side of the coin, along with the words E PLURIBUS UNUM. Also pictured is a small torch of liberty surrounded by a circle of 13 stars representing the 13 colonies or original states.

Half Dollar

Give each child a real and a facsimile half dollar, quarter, dime, nickel, and penny. (If there are many children in the group, you may want to pass one half dollar around and give each child a facsimile only.) As before, have them compare the real and facsimile half dollars, and then compare the half dollars with the other coins.

Heads

The picture on this side shows John F. Kennedy, the thirty-fifth President of the United States, who served from January 20,1961, until his assassination on November 22, 1963. Less than three weeks after Kennedy's death, the new President, Lyndon Johnson, asked Congress for legislation issuing the Kennedy half dollar. Until that time, the half dollar had carried the picture of Benjamin Franklin and was the only coin that did not carry the likeness of a former President of the United States. Have the children find the date the coin was made and the words LIBERTY and IN GOD WE TRUST.

Tails

Have the children turn the coin over to see the picture of an eagle flying. This picture is based on the official seal of the President of the United States. The flying eagle symbolizes victory. In its right claw the eagle carries an olive branch symbolizing peace; in its left it carries 13 arrows symbolizing goodwill (the bow is missing, which means defense by force is a last resort). There are 13 stars above the eagle's head. Let the children use a magnifying glass to count

them. There are also 13 olive leaves, 13 berries, and 13 circular clouds above the eagle, and 13 feathers on each of its wings. This number represents the 13 original states and the 13 signers of the Declaration of Independence. The 50 stars in the ring around the eagle represent the 50 present states. UNITED STATES OF AMERICA and HALF DOLLAR also appear on this side.

Commemorative Half Dollar

The bicentennial half dollar has the dates 1776-1976. The reverse side of the coin shows Independence Hall in Philadelphia, where the Declaration of Independence was signed. The words 200 YEARS OF FREEDOM and E PLURIBUS UNUM appear on the coin. Below the words INDEPENDENCE HALL are 13 stars representing the 13 colonies or original states.

Silver Dollar

The silver dollar is seldom used in everyday money transactions, so it is not included in the activities in this program. However, the following information is included so that you may help the children become familiar with this coin, if you wish to do so.

Heads

The silver dollar issued in 1971 shows a profile view of former President Dwight D. ("Ike") Eisenhower, the thirty-fourth President of the United States. Eisenhower served from 1953 to 1961 and died in 1969. Around the upper rim of the coin are letters spelling LIBERTY, and below Eisenhower's chin are the words IN GOD WE TRUST. The date is at the bottom, and the mint marks are above this.

Tails

The reverse side of the coin commemorates the landing of the Apollo 11 spacecraft "Eagle" on the moon on July 20 and 21, 1969. The silver dollar has a historical tradition of being called the "peace" dollar. Some children may want to read and report on why this is so. Continuing the tradition of the "peace" dollar, the artist, Gasparro, pictures an eagle about to land on the moon's cratered surface while grasping an olive branch signifying peace in its talons. The artist's initials are below the eagle's tail feathers. A small Earth with the outline of the United States is in the upper left.

Commemorative Silver Dollar

The bicentennial silver dollar has the dates 1776-1976 on the front and the Liberty Bell with the moon in the background on the reverse side.

The New One-Dollar Coin

At the time this book was being prepared for publication, the new one-dollar coin was still in the planning stages and had not yet been issued, so it was not included in this program. The new coin will be larger than the quarter and smaller than the half dollar. The reason for the issuance of the new coin is economic: a paper bill has a life of about 18 months, whereas a coin has a life of about 15 years. Also, the dollar coin will be able to be used in vending machines, whereas the dollar bill cannot. Many people want the new coin to commemorate a famous woman. After the coin is issued, you may want to write to the Department of the Treasury, United States Mint, Philadelphia, Pennsylvania 19106, for a complete description of it.

Additional Facts About Coins

The designs on the coins remain in effect for 25 years unless Congress authorizes a change — such as the special designs on the quarter, half dollar, and silver dollar issued to commemorate the bicentennial.

The U.S. Coinage Act of 1965 authorized the reduction of silver content in the dime, quarter, and half dollar. The dime and quarter have an outer layer of 75 percent copper and 25 percent nickel over an inner core of pure copper. The half dollar has an outer layer of 80 percent silver over an inner core of 25 percent silver.

The letter sometimes printed near the date on a coin identifies the mint at which the coin was made. S refers to the San Francisco mint; D, to the Denver mint. If there is no letter, then the coin was made at the Philadelphia mint. (Jefferson nickels minted from 1942 through 1945 carry the letter P to identify the Philadelphia mint.) To discourage hoarding, the mint identifications were omitted from coins minted in 1965, 1966, and 1967. The Philadelphia mint was the first U.S. mint, when that city was the nation's capital. It was so designated by an Act of Congress in April 1792.

Dollar Bills

If possible, give each child a one-dollar bill to examine. At the same time, the children may examine bills of larger denominations to compare likenesses and differences.

The paper bills are called "Federal Reserve Notes." The Federal Reserve System and Federal Reserve Notes were established in 1913. The words FEDERAL RESERVE NOTE are printed at the top of each bill on the front, and below is printed UNITED STATES OF AMERICA. The person pictured in the center of the bill varies with each denomination. Refer to the list on page 11 for the name of the person on each bill. Located at the upper right of the front of the bill and again at the lower left is the bill's serial number. The children will be interested to learn that if a bill is badly torn, a replacement may be obtained at a bank by showing the part with the serial number.

On the right side of the front of any bill is the Treasury Seal, which is superimposed over the word identifying the value of the bill. The Treasury Seal is older than the Constitution, being first adopted by the Continental Congress on September 25, 1778. The newest Seal was adopted in 1968. The design includes a shield on which appears a balance scale symbolizing justice and a key symbolizing authority. Between the two designs is a chevron showing 13 stars. Around the edge are the words THE DEPARTMENT OF THE TREASURY and the date 1789.

The children may notice the very small letters and numbers on the right and left sides of the bill's front. These are the printing plate identification codes. On the bottom right, below the word SERIES, is the year in which the bill was designed.

Of special interest to the children will be the seal with a letter inside, on the left-hand side of the bill, and the single numeral that is printed twice on the right and left sides of the bill. These identify the Federal Reserve District where the bill was first issued. After bills are printed at the Bureau of Engravers and Printers in Washington, D.C., they are shipped to Federal Reserve banks for issue. The children can determine the district in which a bill started its journey into circulation by locating the single numeral on the bill and checking it with the following list. The locations may be checked on a map. The children will find that some bills in their possession have traveled great distances.

Federal Reserve Districts
District 1, Boston, letter A
District 2, New York City, letter B
District 3, Philadelphia, letter C
District 4, Cleveland, letter D
District 5, Richmond, letter E
District 6, Atlanta, letter F
District 7, Chicago, letter G
District 8, St. Louis, letter H
District 9, Minneapolis, letter I
District 10, Kansas City, letter J
District 11, Dallas, letter K
District 12, San Francisco, letter L

Each bill carries a legal tender clause that reads THIS NOTE IS LEGAL TENDER FOR ALL DEBTS, PUBLIC OR PRIVATE. Ask the children to find this on the bills they are examining. In 1957, a law authorized the motto IN GOD WE TRUST on all currency. The children can look for this, too. Each bill is signed by the Treasurer of the United States and the Secretary of the Treasury who were in office at the time the bill was issued. The children may find different names on different bills.

Seven bill denominations are currently in circulation: one dollar, two dollar, five dollar, 10 dollar, 20 dollar, 50 dollar, and 100 dollar. The design of those bills are as follows.

- The **one-dollar bill** has a picture of George Washington on the front and the Great Seal of the United States on the back. The obverse and reverse of the Great Seal first appeared on currency in 1935 on the one-dollar bill. The reverse shows an unfinished pyramid with an eye in triangular glory shining on top of the pyramid. The unfinished pyramid symbolizes that there is yet work to be done. The pyramid is the symbol of strength, and the eye and the triangular glory represent an all-seeing Diety. On the base of the pyramid are the Roman numerals MDCCLXXVI (1776). Some children may be able to interpret the Roman numerals. If not, tell them the date and explain that it is the date of the signing of the Declaration of Independence. Above the eye is the Latin motto ANNUIT COEPTIS, which means "God favored our undertakings." At the bottom is NOVUS ORDO SECLORUM, which means "a new order of the ages." The obverse of the Great Seal shows an eagle with a shield holding an olive branch in one talon and an arrow in the other. Above are 13 stars and the words E PLURIBUS UNUM.

- The **two-dollar bill** issued in 1976 to commemorate the bicentennial has a picture of Thomas Jefferson on the front and a reproduction of John Trumbull's painting showing the signing of the Declaration of Independence in 1776 on the back. The two-dollar bill issued in 1977 has a picture of Jefferson on the front and a picture of his home, Monticello, on the back — the same pictures that are on the nickel.

- The **five-dollar bill** has a picture of Abraham Lincoln on the front and a picture of the Lincoln Memorial on the back — the same pictures that are on the penny.

- The **10-dollar bill** has a picture of Alexander Hamilton (the first Secretary of the Treasury) on the front and a picture of the Treasury Building on the back.

- The **20-dollar bill** has a picture of Andrew Jackson (the seventh President of the United States) on the front and a picture of the White House on the back.

- The **50-dollar bill** has a picture of Ulysses S. Grant (the eighteenth President of the United States) on the front and a picture of the Capitol Building on the back.

- The **100-dollar bill** has a picture of Benjamin Franklin on the front and a picture of Independence Hall in Philadelphia on the back.

For exchanges of large amounts of money involving 500 dollars or more, bank checks are used rather than paper bills. Beginning in 1969, the government has slowly withdrawn the larger bills from circulation. On the back of the larger bills are ornate words and numerals stating their value. The people pictured on the front of the bills are as follows.

- The **500-dollar bill** has a picture of William McKinley, the twenty-fifth President of the United States.

- The **1,000-dollar bill** has a picture of Grover Cleveland, the twenty-second and twenty-fourth President.

- The **5,000-dollar bill** has a picture of James Madison, the fourth President.

- The **10,000-dollar bill** has a picture of Salmon P. Chase, a Secretary of the Treasury and a Chief Justice.

- The **100,000-dollar bill** has a picture of Woodrow Wilson, the twenty-eighth President.

Special Printing Process

The process of printing paper money begins with a skilled engraver who cuts the design into a steel plate. This plate is used to press the design onto the rollers of the presses. The roller then presses the design into hundreds of printing plates that are used to print the bills. The very special processes used are intended to prevent the printing of counterfeit money. The making of the special paper and the ink is a secret process that is carefully guarded. The paper contains tiny blue and red threads that can be seen in new bills. The paper is 75 percent cotton and 25 percent linen.

Additional Activities

Research Projects

Older children may enjoy doing research projects based on the coins and bills. Have the children look in reference books for additional information about the people, places, and symbols shown on coins and bills, and write short

reports about them. Or they may want to do research into the coins and bills themselves or find out about U.S. currency in the past. Some children may have coin collections of their own that they could show and tell the other children about. These projects could be used as ways of earning money in the classroom economy.

Genuine or Counterfeit?

As part of the research projects or as a separate activity, older children may enjoy finding out about ways to identify counterfeit bills. An excellent booklet titled "Counterfeit?" is available from the Research Department, Federal Reserve Bank of Atlanta, 104 Marietta Street, N.W., Atlanta, Georgia 30303. Order a copy of the booklet for each child in your group. You also should have several real bills available for study.

Give each child a copy of the booklet, and then read and study it together. The booklet describes several distinctive clues that can be used in identifying counterfeit bills and tells what to do if you get a counterfeit bill.

A Classroom Economy

A Classroom Economy

Introduction

After the coins and the one-dollar bill have been introduced through the activities in the previous section, you may begin the classroom economy. However, it is *not* necessary that all coins and the dollar bill be included in the economy at the beginning. With very young children or children at a beginning level, you may want to begin the economy using only the penny. With other children, you may want to start with only the penny and nickel, or only the penny, nickel, and dime. The remaining coins may be introduced one by one later, using the introductory activities described in the previous section, and then incorporated into the ongoing economy.

Many different kinds of activities are suggested in this section. Select activities and adjust the procedures to meet the needs and abilities of your particular group. Also feel free to incorporate your own ideas or ideas that the children themselves may suggest.

Materials Needed

Coins and Bills

You will need an ample supply of facsimile coins and bills for the classroom economy. The number of coins and bills of each denomination will depend on which ones you are using in the economy and the number of children participating. As a general guideline, you may want to start with about 25 of each of the lower-value coins and 10 of each of the higher-value coins and the bills for a small group of children. Adjust the quantity if necessary as the economy progresses. If you introduce coins on a gradual basis, you will need about 25 or more pennies for each child.

You may use commercially available sets of facsimile money such as Teaching Resources' *Coins and Bills.* (This set includes 24 pennies, 24 nickels, 24 dimes, 12 quarters, 12 half dollars, 16 one-dollar bills, 12 five-dollar bills, eight 10-dollar bills, four 20-dollar bills, four 50-dollar bills, and four 100-dollar bills.) You may want to laminate the bills between two sheets of clear contact paper. Lay down one sheet of contact paper with the adhesive side up. Arrange the bills side by side on the sheet. Then carefully lower the second sheet over the bills, adhesive side down. Smooth out any bubbles and wrinkles, and then cut out the bills with scissors. Laminating the bills ensures that they will last indefinitely without being torn. Otherwise, in a classroom economy, their life would be short.

You also could make your own facsimile money to use either instead of or in addition to purchased sets of coins and bills. The coins could be printed with stamps such as Teaching Resources' *Coin Stamps: Heads and Tails.* Stamps for bills are also available commercially. Print each coin on a small square of construction paper — light brown for the pennies, light gray for the other coins. Print the bills on light green construction paper. Let the children do the printing themselves, since this helps them become more familiar with the coins and bills. They also could trim the prints so the paper coins are circular like real coins. The paper coins and bills will wear out quickly in the classroom economy, but they are easy and inexpensive to replace. Printing coins and bills yourself also guarantees that you will have an ample supply at all times, particularly of the lower-value coins if you are beginning the economy with only those.

Class Bank

You will need one tray or shallow box with compartments, for use as the class bank. The bank should have at least six compartments — one for the bills and one for each of the

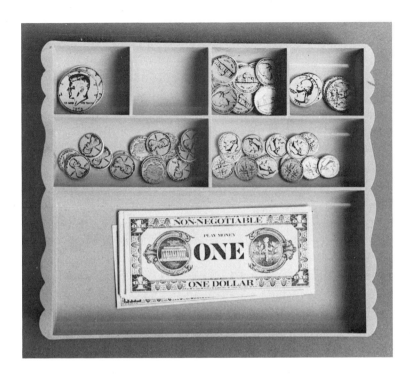

Explaining the System

At the initial set-up time, explain the system's rules, guidelines, and expectations so the children will understand how they get their money and how they spend it. Specific activities and ways for the children to earn and spend money are suggested later in this section. At this point, simply give the children a general overview of the system. This will help the economy run smoothly.

Explain that you will pay them for certain classwork, special assignments, regular classroom jobs, good behavior, and many other things. Decide ahead of time whether you want to pay them daily, weekly, or bi-weekly, and tell the children how often you will pay them.

Explain that the money they earn belongs only to them and is to be kept in their personal banks. No one is allowed to touch the money in anyone else's bank. Tell the children that they can count their money to see how much they have, and that they can use their money to buy things from a class store, rent things, buy privileges, and many other things.

Show the children the class bank, and explain that this is the bank to which they pay money when they buy or rent something. Tell them that the class bank is to be used only by you (or an aide) or by a child who has been specifically designated as the "banker" for a period of time.

denominations of coins. Keeping the coins and bills in separate compartments facilitates payments and making change by you or by children designated as "bankers."

Personal Banks

Each child will need a small container to hold his or her money. The container could be a box with an attached lid, such as a schoolbox or a cigar box, or a plastic freezer container or a coffee can with a snap-on lid, or even a small purse. Whatever the container a child uses, it should be small enough to fit in his or her desk but large enough to hold bills without bending or crumpling them. In a special session, let each child personalize his or her bank by decorating it in any way he or she chooses.

Payments and Prices

When you assign values to things the children can do to earn money and when you price items that the children can buy, assign values according to the children's ability level and in a way that helps them learn money values in easy stages. For example, begin with payments and prices of even amounts: 5¢, 10¢, 25¢, 50¢, and $1. Use 75¢ later when the children become more adept at handling money. Gradually introduce amounts that require the children to add coin values: for example, 17¢, 42¢, 86¢.

From the beginning, you also may include payments and prices from $2 to $10 or more. However, you should use even dollar amounts initially. Since it is sometimes a long while before most children become accustomed to reading prices and understanding values, it seems to confuse them if you use payments or prices such as $1.10 and $3.25. Begin with whole-dollar amounts such as $3.00 or $7.00. When these are well understood, introduce the half dollar with amounts such as $1.50. Then introduce amounts such as $1.10 and $3.25. Increase the difficulty of the payments and prices by slow, careful stages. If you use the classroom economy throughout the entire school year, there is ample time for the children to practice their skills and progress in easy stages.

If you are using only the penny in the initial stages of the economy, payments and prices may range from 1¢ to 25¢ or higher, depending on the range of values you want the children to learn. When you begin paying the children, make all payments in pennies. They will quickly learn their counting skills because they will want to know how much money they have. When handling pennies is fully comprehended by the children, add the nickel to the economy. Pay the children in nickels and pennies, and give a nickel in exchange when a child has five pennies. Price items in multiples of five: 5¢, 10¢, 15¢, 20¢, and so on. This will quickly lead to the need to introduce the dime and quarter into the economy and later the half dollar and one-dollar bill. If you use the penny system, it is suggested that the other coins be added as soon as possible. Experience has shown that children working on a first-grade level can learn to handle all five coins very quickly in a classroom economy, even if they have never handled the coins before.

Counting and Changing Money

Getting a little money in their personal banks as a start is important. The first payment might be 10 cents to each child for having made such an attractive bank. Any money earned the first day is handled, looked at, and remembered by the children. If they are just learning money, then the first day it would be important to find ways to pay each

child several pennies that could be changed for a nickel or several nickels that could be changed for a dime or quarter.

When the economy first begins, the children will probably count their money individually at every opportunity throughout the day. This should be allowed, as it enhances their counting and mental arithmetic skills quickly. In fact, experience has shown that even when the system has been used for months, most children can tell you at any given moment exactly how much they have in their banks.

This stage of counting their money practically all day long is usually excessive for only the first week or two of the classroom economy. Some teachers say they cannot use the system because the children are busy counting their money when they should be doing other work. Even though you appreciate the children's enthusiasm, it may be necessary to ask them to leave their money in their desks until a task or lesson is finished. The excessive counting of money usually wears off in a few weeks. If it does not, you may want to set aside a special time each day for counting and changing money. This could be during the regular math lesson, immediately before or after lunch, or at the beginning or end of the school day. The repeated money-counting is well worth whatever inconvenience it may cause. The children are highly motivated and are acquiring an invaluable skill.

For beginners, changing money should be a structured activity. Have each child stack his or her pennies into piles of five pennies each. Then, working with one child at a time, explain and demonstrate that each pile of five pennies can be exchanged for one nickel, two nickels can be exchanged for a dime, two dimes and a nickel can be exchanged for a quarter, and so forth. Work slowly and always explain what you are doing in detail. Most beginners will feel poorer with one dime in place of ten pennies. Many children will be very reluctant to change their money, especially if they had 10 pennies, one nickel, and one dime, and now all they have is one coin, a quarter. If you meet with too much resistance, then do not insist that all of their money be changed. Resistance can be overcome by praising those who have a half dollar or a one-dollar bill. At a later time, when the children are more familiar with coin values, praise those who have bills of higher denominations, such as a five-, 10-, or 20-dollar bill. Every so often, find out who has the most money and express enthusiasm.

Assign children who have become accomplished in money-counting skills to help others. The time spent in changing money from lower-value coins to higher-value coins will benefit the child's skills and shorten the learning time.

Changing money in a structured activity will take longer at first than simply doing the changing for the children, but they will quickly learn how to do it themselves. Soon the children will be able to arrange piles of coins on their desks quickly and say, "I'd like one dollar for this pile, and a quarter for this, and a five-dollar bill for these."

Some children may need to change their nickels and dimes into two quarters before they realize they have a half dollar, or their pennies into nickels and their nickels into dimes and so on before they realize they have one dollar. These children need a tremendous amount of repetition and experience in counting money. That is why it is important to allow the children to count their money every day and to continue the classroom economy throughout the year. Otherwise, there is no other way for the children to get this needed experience and be motivated, too.

Potential Problems

This point should be emphasized right at the beginning, on the first day you start the classroom economy: *no one is to take any money from the class bank or from anyone else's bank.* Explain that anyone who is guilty of this will probably have all of his or her money taken away and will have to start over again. If you have a class store or other display of items for sale or rent, explain that taking things without paying for them will be treated in the same way. The person who has taken an item will have all of his or her money taken away.

Due to personal developmental problems, it may be difficult for some children to understand what you mean. Such children will have to be watched carefully and reminded

often about what is correct. If these children forget and are seen taking money or items, they should immediately be told, "No," and directed to put the money or items back themselves. They can be paid as a reward for remembering and telling you that money in the class bank and in other children's banks is not to be touched, and items in the class store are not to be taken. If the children understand but take money or items anyway, then withhold money from them for the rest of the day.

Experience in using the classroom economy has shown that some children will knowingly take money from the class bank or from other children's banks. The best procedure to insure that this does not happen again has been to confront the child, tell him or her what was wrong, say that this is a serious thing to do, and tell the child that he or she must give up all of his or her own money. If the child has saved 50 dollars, then a large fine may be enough to solve the problem on the first offense.

When the system is used over a full school year, the "takings" by one or two children may be subtle. You or the other children may wonder (or even ask aloud), "How did they get so much money?" When someone who has been suspected for a long time is finally caught, it is best to follow the same procedure and take all the child's savings away. Confronting the child privately, exacting total payment, and then never mentioning it again seems to be the most helpful way to deal with these situations. In most cases, the incident should be looked on very lightly. No child should be labeled a "thief" by you or the class.

A less serious offense is defacing money. Explain to the class that this is not allowed with real money, and that they will not be allowed to write on or mark their classroom money or tear it up. If it should happen, then the child would lose his or her defaced money.

Earning Money

There are many, many ways for the children to earn money in the classroom economy. These are some suggestions that have been tried with several classes. You will undoubtedly develop methods for your own classroom according to the children's needs and abilities. In the meantime, you may find some ideas among these that have already been used.

- When the children are doing their reading and phonics work, small payments of pennies and nickels encourage them to do their best. An alternative method to passing out money during lesson time is to keep track of points and then pay the children when the lesson is over.

- Pay the children for doing their best oral reading.

- Pay them for taking part in activities. This will encourage shy children to take part, and the ones who were previously indifferent may have new enthusiasm.

- For certain activities, tell the children ahead of time how much they will earn. Then pay each child the same amount when the activity is accomplished. Give a certain amount to those children who finish their work, but pay more if the work is neat. Pay less for unfinished work, but do not fine anyone for messy or unfinished work; those papers are simply worth less. Tell the child the reason for less pay or no pay at all.

- Pay for homework handed in. If the work was time-consuming, pay more. Do not fine children for not bringing in homework. If several children do not bring in their work, then pay a high amount to those who do their work in order to make it very worthwhile. Tell the child who does not do the work that you will pay for late work but not the full price.

- For class learning games in which teams are chosen, pay everyone on the winning team the highest amount and pay everyone on the other team or teams a lesser amount.

- Pay a child for successful work in another classroom if he or she is cross-grouped on a regular basis.

- Pay a particular amount for each arithmetic example that is correct or for each page completed. If there is a full page of arithmetic examples and you are paying 50 cents for the page, then deduct a certain amount for each example that is incorrect before paying the child.

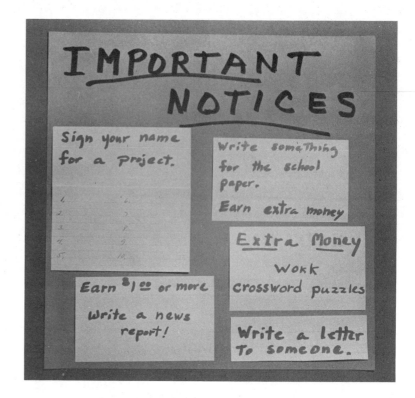

- Pay for perfect spelling papers. Keep a record, and pay one dollar to any child who has 10 perfect spelling papers.

- For vocabulary work, pay a child for each word known.

- Pay for extra work done. Put up notices about extra work and how much can be earned.

- Pay for written or oral news reports.

- Pay for write-ups on items of interest that the children have copied from a book or newspaper.

- Pay one cent a word for original stories or poems about real or imagined experiences. You may want to suggest topics such as "What I Can Do Best" or "My Favorite Sport."

- Pay for a letter written to someone.

- Pay for the telling of an interesting fact or for the sharing of an interesting experience with the class.

- Encourage environmental projects for pay such as picking up trash, collecting cans and bottles, or cleaning or clearing areas.

- Pay those with neat desks, and give no payment to those with messy desks.

- Every now and then, have a class password. Pay those who remember the password when they come into the classroom in the morning or after recess. The password may pertain to a study unit. For example, if the word "thermometer" were the password, each child would have to name it and tell what it does.

- Pay those who bring in an item that pertains to a particular season or a particular study unit. Originality and creativity are fostered: one child may bring in a fallen leaf for autumn, another child may draw a picture, and another may bring in a picture cut from a magazine or a book with pictures.

The children themselves will think of interesting ways to earn extra money if you encourage it and discuss it with them. These experiences can enrich their lives as well as their bank accounts.

Contracts

Contracts are another way for the children to earn money. A contract is a written agreement between you and a child that he or she will achieve some specified goal by a specified date. The goal may be behavioral or academic. If the child achieves the goal by the specified date, then the child receives payment.

Prepare many blank contracts, or make a contract on a spirit master so you can run off multiple copies. You may want to leave space around the borders so the child can illustrate or decorate his or her contract. Fill in the terms of the contract, and discuss the task, date, and payment with the child so the contract has real meaning. When the terms are satisfactory to both you and the child, then you each

sign the contract. The child is responsible for meeting the terms of the contract and for presenting it to you for payment on the date agreed upon.

```
┌─────────────────────────────────────────┐
│                                          │
│   I will _____  │
│                                          │
│   _____  │
│                                          │
│   _____  │
│                                          │
│   by this date _____  │
│                                          │
│   payment earned _____  │
│                                          │
│   _____  │
│              (student's signature)       │
│                                          │
│   _____  │
│              (teacher's signature)       │
│                                          │
└─────────────────────────────────────────┘
```

Different contracts may be written for different children. Also, any one child may have several contracts to work on at the same time. The contract is an excellent tool for helping a child realize what his or her goals may be and in working toward achieving those goals.

Special Person

Designate one area of the bulletin board as the "Special Spot" and choose one child each day to be the "Special Person." Print or write the child's name on a sheet of paper, and decorate it with a colorful border. A small photograph of the child also could be included. Post the paper in the "Special Spot." Assign a particular academic or behavioral task to the child, such as successful participation in a reading group, completion of a math assignment by a specified time, or playing fairly at recess. If the child completes the task, then he or she earns an extra amount of money for himself or herself and for each member of the class. This activity is helpful in promoting positive self-concepts and peer relationships. If a child feels pressured by being the "Special Person" with a task to complete, assign that child a task that you know he or she can accomplish without difficulty. With another child, the awareness of the other children's expectations may provide a motivating challenge and help the child do his or her best.

Paychecks

With more capable children, you may want to assign classroom jobs on a weekly or bi-weekly basis and then pay the children by "check" at the end of the period. One of the job assignments could be the "secretary" who is responsible for writing down each child's name, job assignment, dates of the assignment, and salary. A "treasurer" could be responsible for issuing the checks.

Prepare many blank checks, or make a check on a spirit master so you can run off multiple copies. At the end of each pay period, you or the "treasurer" should make out a check for each child. The children can endorse their checks and cash them at the class bank. Or you may want to use the "direct deposit" system: tell the children that their paychecks have been deposited in the bank, and let them write checks to withdraw all or part of the amount in cash. You could designate one day each week as banking day for these transactions.

This procedure works particularly well with older children. The children learn how to write, endorse, and cash checks, and also learn the value of checks in a real economy.

			19____
Pay to the order of _____		$_____	
_____ Dollars			
(name of bank)			
_____			
for _____			

Spending Money

As with earning money, there are many ways for the children to spend money in a classroom economy. Several projects that have proven to be appealing and successful are suggested on the following pages. Feel free to add your own activities as well.

A Class Store

Setting Up the Store

Any small area in the classroom can become the site for a class store. A table and several shelves or a windowsill could make an attractive setting. Let the children take part in setting up the store.

Discuss the store with the children, and then send a note home to their parents. With the parents' permission, the children may be able to bring things from home that otherwise would be discarded. Donated items can be used to stock the store.

Here is one example of a note that might be sent home. You may want to give each child several copies of the note so he or she can pass it out to other relatives and friends as well. Each child should sign his or her name to the note.

Dear Parents and Other Interested Persons,

We have a store in our classroom. This helps us learn our money skills. The money we use looks just like it is real, and we get paid for things that we do.

We would welcome donations to our store anytime during the school year. We would accept anything, especially children's books, jewelry, perfume or cologne bottles (used or empty), pretty boxes or other small containers, games, notions, toys appropriate for all ages, pictures, old calendars, and anything else. Thank you.

From,

Not all items donated to the store need be for children. A great part of the time, the children will buy things from the store to give as gifts to adults — parents, other relatives, teachers, or aides. Try to maintain a wide variety of items in the store. Make a good supply of the notes, and send one or more copies home with each child several times during the year so the store is always well-stocked.

As an added service, it is nice to have some big squares or sheets of colorful tissue paper or other wrapping paper, clear tape, ribbon or colored yarn, and small tags or cards so the children can wrap gifts they buy. Charge a small amount (10 or 25 cents) for the gift-wrapping service.

Personal Sales

Some children may bring in their good toys or other things from home and try to sell them to other children in the class. Emphasize the policy that they may donate things to the store, but they should not sell their things from home and collect the money themselves. Discuss this policy with the children when you are sending the note home.

Safety

Before putting donated items into the store, check each item carefully for health-and-safety features. Discard any items that are broken or unusually dirty, have sharp edges, or smell musty with mildew. Some children may be buying things for younger brothers and sisters at home, so check each item for exposed nails or wires and for peeling paint. Paint should be nontoxic, and plastic parts should be shatterproof. Throw out anything that looks suspicious. (As an added precaution, throw out items after the children have left school for the day, as they have a way of finding things in the wastebasket.)

Pricing Items

In pricing items for the store, follow the general guidelines given in *Payments and Prices*, pages 15-16. The pricing of the merchandise will probably be up to you, but new articles can always be shown to the class and a price discussed with them. What the item might have cost new and its condition now should determine the price.

Once the price of an item is established, make a price tag for it. For beginning students, you may want to make large price tags and mark the price in numerals and in stamped pictures of the exact amount in coins, so the children can match their coins to the ones on the tag. The children could prepare the price tags themselves.

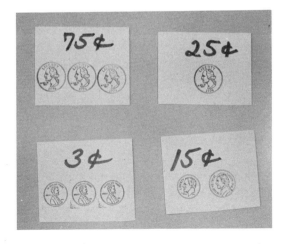

You or the children may want to set up the store so that all items selling for one price are together in one box — one box for items costing one cent, another for items costing five cents, and so on. (If you are wondering what could sell for only one or two cents, decorative stickers could, and they are very popular with children.)

Staffing the Store

One child could be in charge of sales, collect the money, and make change for one week at a time. This child may receive a "salary" at the end of the week for the time the store was open during the five weekdays. During the week, a team of two or three other children could straighten the merchandise or arrange it according to their own taste. These children also may receive "salaries."

Store Hours

The store may be open for a certain amount of time once each day. Convenient times may be mid-morning or the half hour before or after lunch. The children may browse and look at the items during their free time. Having regular store times is the fairest way to open the store. This allows for a concentrated activity period that can be administered by the children taking turns collecting money and being the salesperson. The store activities become more meaningful on a once-a-day basis and are less distracting to the regular curriculum. An auction may be held once a week during this time. Also, IOU's and lay-away activities could be taken care of during store time. Sometimes, buying and selling can be very active, and it is a good idea to have a timer that rings when the day's money activities are to come to an end. All unfinished business can be resumed another day.

Lay-Away Plan

The children will soon learn that they can waste money and that they must make decisions about articles they really want. Otherwise, they will often find themselves "broke" and unable to pay for an article or privilege they want. This can be remedied by the lay-away plan.

Suppose someone has donated to the store a beautiful grass bag from some exotic place, which is just what a certain child wants but cannot afford. Accept as much as the child can afford as a down-payment. Make a note of the full price and the child's down-payment on a card, along with the child's name, and attach the card to the item. Put the object in view but not in the store. Let the child pay off the balance bit by bit. Each time the child makes a payment, cross out the previous balance and write the new balance.

When the item is completely paid for, the child may take it. If the child has lost interest in the item before he or she has made final payment, refund the child's money. (If a child abuses the lay-away privilege by repeatedly putting items on lay-away and then changing his or her mind and not paying for them, you may have to charge the child a small "service charge" or even make the down-payments nonrefundable. Explain that this is what stores do in real life.)

IOU's

If a child cannot quite afford an item and its price is low, then an IOU may be preferable to the lay-away plan.

On a file card, write IOU in big letters, the amount owed, and the child's name. Let the child take the item. Put the card in a place where it can be seen easily as a reminder to you and the child. The child will probably pay up as soon as he or she has earned the needed money. Write PAID on the card and give it to the child. He or she may either discard it or keep it as a souvenir.

Reselling Items

In all cases, sales should be final after a reasonable length of time. Sometimes a child may tire of a nice article he or she bought from the store and may want to offer it for resale at his or her own asking price. Allow time for this during store hours. With this practice, the children will get a "feel" for how much they think something is worth and how much they want to pay for something considering its condition.

If no one wants to buy the item, then you could make the child an offer to buy it with money from the class bank and recycle it back into the store. Items that are left around or returned to you by other teachers may be put away and recycled into the store at a later date when they may not be recognized any more.

There may be many children who buy items simply because they have the money. For example, one child may want to sell a broken toy he or she once bought from the store for 50 cents. Several children may offer to buy it just because they have 50 cents. Others may want to buy it just because they like the child selling the item. It may be helpful to these children to ask that the object be passed around so those interested may examine it closely, and to ask each child if he or she really wants the item. Explain that it is important to make good decisions on how to spend money.

Auctions

Auctions are a lot of fun for the children, and many math skills can be learned and practiced if the bidding is guided and structured by you. Some teachers have used auctions even with children in first grade.

The items to be auctioned may consist of some items from the store and some donated expressly for the auction. You also may want to auction off a mystery box containing a Zonk (something of little or no value) or a Bonanza (something of value or appeal). It is best to be very selective about the objects in the mystery box if it is to be a Zonk. A Zonk might be some item from the store that is not selling well or a collection of small objects that are not worth much, such as a balloon, a pencil, a nickel or quarter in facsimile currency, an old calendar, and so forth. Put enough in the box so the winning bidder will not feel bad. If the Zonk is worthless, it will discourage others from bidding on mystery boxes on other days. For a Bonanza, put in more facsimile money as well as more valuable or appealing items such as gum, a special-privilege coupon, or something "good" from the store. One mystery box per auction is sufficient.

Before the auction begins, announce how the bidding will go. With beginners who are learning to count, the bidding can start at one cent and increase one cent with each bid. Each child must listen and figure out how much is one more than the previous bid. Or start at two or three cents and have the children increase the bids by twos or threes. With more capable children, you may want to start at five cents and increase the bidding by fives. The five-times table is learned quickly this way. Increasing the bids by tens is popular. At other times, increase the bid by 25's or 50's. If the bidding gets up to several dollars, remind the children that they must have the money before they bid. As they bid, you might ask each child if he or she has the money.

The mystery box is the item that probably will be greeted with the most excitement and interest. Encourage bidding, but remind the children that the box may contain either a Zonk or a Bonanza and that they will not know which it is until the winning bidder opens the box. (It is best to let the *child* decide which it is; he or she may think the opposite of what you thought!) If there are several small objects in the box, give the child a chance to offer for sale anything he or she does not want. It will be interesting to see the price the child will ask for an item and then to see if anyone will buy it. Other children are quick to express their opinion if they feel someone is being cheated.

Auctions are very popular, and you probably will want to hold one fairly often (but not so often that it loses its novelty). Between auctions, encourage the children to save their money so they may bid at the next one. You also may want to visit a "real" auction with your class, or encourage the children to visit one with their families. Explain that used items often can be bought for bargain prices at auctions.

Draw a Number

Put a number on each book for sale in the store or on other items. Write a matching number on a small card or square of paper. Put these numbers in a unique container such as a woven basket or a shiny L'Eggs container. Shake the container and mix the numbers well.

Announce that for 50 cents (or whatever amount you feel is appropriate), anyone who wants to may draw a number and get a surprise present from the store. Explain that one of the numbers will be for an item that is much more valuable than 50 cents. The children may be told which item it is. Each child pays, draws a number, and then looks for that number on the store items to see what he or she has won. When everyone who wants to participate has drawn a number, the container and remaining numbers may be saved for another time.

It is most effective to put numbers on the books for sale in the store because books rarely move in a voluntary purchase. When the children win books, they seem to enjoy them. They like the game and will ask that it be played again.

Door Prizes

When you are having a special occasion or a class party, sell chances on door prizes. Exhibit the items beforehand, and make a sign reading *Buy a Chance! Only $1.00!* (or whatever amount you think is appropriate). Each child buying a chance puts his or her name on a slip of paper and puts the paper in a box next to the item he or she wants. When the time comes for the drawing, mix up the names in the box and let a child draw one name for each prize. It is an enjoyable experience for the children to take chances on prizes, and they will learn what to do in similar real-life experiences.

Guessing Game

For a party or other special occasion, fill a small, clear container with small edible items such as gumdrops, M&M's, pieces of popcorn, or nuts. Count the items, then replace them in the container and close the lid tightly. Sell chances

small peep show with 15 containers

for 50 cents (or whatever amount you think is appropriate). Each child who buys a chance writes his or her name on a slip of paper and the number of items he or she thinks is in the container. Collect all the slips of paper, look at the numbers the children guessed, and give the container of items to the child whose number is closest to the actual number you counted. The winner can count the items so everyone else can see. This activity helps the children learn to estimate numbers.

Peep Show

Collect a number of containers with lids, such as plastic margarine tubs, coffee cans, and baby food jars. Put one or more interesting items in each container, and put on the lid. Label each lid with a title that tells what is in the container and a price needed to see or use the item. Titles and items are suggested below.

Work a Puzzle (small picture puzzle)
Work a Puppet (small hand puppet or finger puppet)
Use Some Perfume (perfume salve)
Try On Rings (several different rings)
Spin a Top (small top)
Use a Magnifying Glass (small magnifying glass and interesting objects such as stamps)
See a Skeleton (small rubber skeleton)
Car (toy car)
Bugs (small rubber bugs)

larger peep show with 26 containers

Noisemaker (small horn, whistle, clicker, or party noise-maker)

Brain Teaser (small puzzle)

Odds and Ends (gears, screws, nuts and bolts, or other interesting items)

Mirrors (several small mirrors or one larger one)

Put the peep show box on display, and let each child rent a container of his or her choice for a period of time. If the peep show is used with a small group, have each child show you the correct amount of money before he or she takes the container. Not looking into the container until the correct amount of money has been paid creates suspense, mystery, and interest.

Special-Privilege Coupons

Make and sell coupons for special privileges such as 15 minutes of free time to work on a model or play a game. (The activities must be ones that do not disturb others.) Post a sign listing the privileges the children can buy. You may run off copies of coupons with a space for a child's name. When a child buys a coupon, his or her name may be written on it. The child may keep the coupon until he or she is ready to use it.

Renting

Renting items is another way of giving the children an opportunity to spend their money. Rent games or equipment for recess time. Rent games, books, or magazines to take home for the weekend. Rent (or sell) pencils to children who lose theirs. Many opportunities special to your classroom and school will present themselves.

Paying Bills

With older children, you may want to bill the children for things they use during the week. Charge a fee for use of desks, books, pencils, maps, and other classroom equipment and supplies. Make up a bill for each child, and designate one day of the week as bill-paying day. Insist on

proper budgeting so the children can pay their weekly bills. When a child's bill is paid on time, mark *paid* on it. Charge a 10 percent late fee. This activity helps the children learn how to plan and budget their money, and relates directly to real-life experiences.

Saving Money

It is good to provide an alternative to spending by encouraging saving money. Stimulate the children's interest in saving money by offering special activities from time to time (auctions, peep shows, and the like) for which they must save. Give them a real reason for using willpower, trying not to waste their money, and spending wisely. Help them discover that there is something better than instant gratification and being "broke" at the end of each day.

With older children, you may want to set up savings accounts. Explain the advantages of a savings account, and discuss the difference between a savings account and a regular checking account. Make up spirit masters with deposit and withdrawal slips and a bank book. Set aside a day and time each week for deposits and withdrawals from the children's accounts. Let each child fill out the proper slips.

Compute interest every week, every month, every two months, or as often as you would like the children to practice this skill. Making deposits and withdrawals and computing interest helps the children develop math skills that relate directly to real-life experience.

WITHDRAWAL FROM ACCOUNT

Account No. _____   Date _____ 19 ____

in cash   [_____]

AMOUNT

[_____]

Write out amount.

Name _____

DEPOSIT TO ACCOUNT

Account No. _____   Date _____ 19 ____

Name _____

	AMOUNT	
Cash		
Check		
Total		

SAVINGS ACCOUNT

Account No. _____

Name _____

Date	Deposits	Withdrawals	Interest	Balance

Classroom Management

The classroom economy helps motivate the children toward desirable attitudes in learning and in relating to others. It is a reward system that the children learn to like more and more as the school year progresses, and it is a system that works remarkably well because there are so many interesting things to do with the money earned.

With this system each child can be rewarded individually, which is the fairest type of reward. As the system becomes an integral part of the classroom, it helps give a teacher control. If prices and payments are fair — and they can always be discussed openly with the children so they are in agreement — then the children will do spelling, math, or other academic tasks for payment. The system lends itself to instant payment, if needed.

Some additional suggestions are: Praise along with payment encourages good work and extra work. Praise the children on their earnings and savings. Reward work when it is done well, and pay less for poor work.

An added motivator for a child may be to tape a half dollar or a dollar bill on a post or the wall, in the child's view. In this way, the child sees the reward for which he or she is working, and the child's efforts to complete work will usually be successful.

Another way of rewarding is to show the child four quarters and then put them in constant view of the child. Let the child know that the money will be his or hers at some specified time. If some undesirable behavior occurs, remove one quarter. This type of behavior-management technique works well because the money does not yet belong to the child. This reward method helps the child work from within himself or herself to achieve desirable behavior.

It is not good for a child's self-esteem to post lists of names of children who misbehave and to label the reasons. The classroom economy can become a behavior-management program that is both individualized and comfortable for the children. Do not take money from a child unless it is a bona fide fine such as a "late" fee for not returning a rented

item on time. Sometimes, for a flagrant misdemeanor, an on-the-spot fine may be the only effective recourse. Tell the child that you are fining him or her a specific amount of money and that he or she can pay the fine now or whenever he or she is able. To avoid a confrontation, write the amount on a card and put it within the child's view, or tape it out of reach with the comment that his or her debt will be erased the very moment he or she pays.

Another time when it is all right to take money from a child is when there has been a previous agreement, such as, "When we have desk inspection this afternoon, I will pay you fifty cents for a neat desk. If the desk is messy, then you have to pay me fifty cents." This gives the child plenty of time to get ready and makes a game out of the activity.

Concentrate the classroom economy on rewarding for money earned, and ignore certain behavior or unfinished work because the reward is no payment. This is all the fine most children will need because they will want to earn money in order to enjoy the many extras that are offered.

Ending the Economy

Care should be given to ending the economy because it has become an integral part of the classroom structure, academically and affectively. It is difficult for a child to give up his or her money, so care should be taken in severing the children from this expression of themselves. Wait until the last possible day, and then dissolve their accounts with goods in exchange for their money. If the experience is pleasurable, then the let-down is lessened.

Discuss the termination of the economy a few days ahead of time. Solicit their ideas, and let them know and plan for the way they want to give up all their money. The rule is, all money must go. Several possibilities are:

- Allow time for a last splurge at the class store.
- Auction several items in the mystery box.
- Bring in a bag of goodies, and sell each item for 50 cents.

- Have a goodbye party, and sell chances on door prizes. At one dollar per chance, it is all right if someone takes 35 chances!

When their money is gone, have a discussion about how they liked earning and spending money all year.

Some children in the class may have been quite wealthy for the entire time the economy was in operation. Others may have lived from one IOU to the next. Some will have spent all their money instantly, and others will have saved and stashed their money away in several containers. In short, the classroom economy will have been a microcosm of society. The economy will have provided an excellent opportunity for the children to develop an understanding of how people get money in real life and how it goes, either wisely or foolishly.

Having a classroom economy is a true simulation game that can be carried on for the full school year without any abatement of class enthusiasm. With the variety of activities used in the economy, the children's enthusiasm only mounts as the school year progresses and their ability to handle money increases. Classroom friendships seem to increase, and the learning atmosphere is heightened. There is no such thing as boredom with or disinterest in learning money skills, and by the end of the school year those children who once could not recognize a coin are now adept at handling money. It is a wonderful transition for a teacher to watch, and you realize that the economy is more than worth the extra time and work. It has probably stimulated an interest in saving money and given the children a real reason for trying to spend wisely and not waste their money. It may have helped them discover that there is something better than instant gratification. Through the classroom economy, in just one school year the children will have achieved many long-lasting goals that will be useful throughout life.

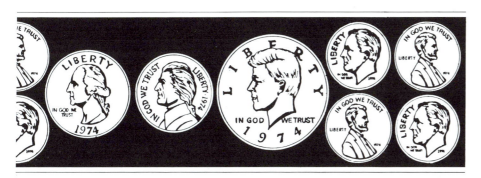

Supplementary Activities and Games

Coin Cookies

Materials Needed

ingredients for sugar cookies (your own recipe) *or* one bag
    of sugar cookie mix plus butter and one egg *or* one or
    two rolls of frozen sugar cookie dough (see Advance
    Preparations)
waxed paper
tape
flour
set of coin cookie cutters (see Advance Preparations)
knives, Popsicle sticks, or art sticks
small brush
cookie sheet
oven

cookies after baking

Advance Preparations

Your supermarket may carry the coin cookie cutters made
by Wecolite. If not, order them from Wecolite Company,
Inc., Teaneck, New Jersey 07666. The cutters print realistic
pictures of the heads of a quarter, half dollar, penny, and
dime and the face of a two-dollar bill. No nickel cutter is
included. The children may make their own nickel impression in the dough.

Prepare the cookie dough either from your own recipe or
from the mix. If you are using the frozen dough, let it thaw
at room temperature.

Directions

Tape a sheet of waxed paper to each child's work surface.
Show the children how to rub flour on the waxed paper so
the dough will not stick to it. Then give each child a small
amount of cookie dough, just enough to make a round ball
for one coin. The child may roll the dough between his or
her hands or on the waxed paper. Then the child presses the
ball with the palm of his or her hand to make a flat circle
about ⅜ inch in thickness.

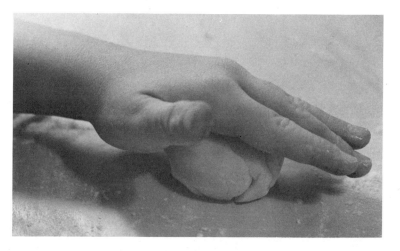

rolling the dough

32

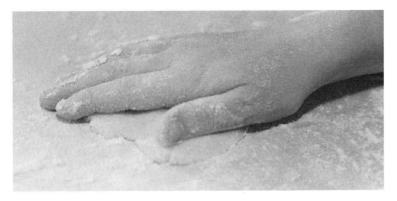

flattening the dough

removing the cutter

Next, the child chooses one of the cutters, dips it in the flour (it also may be necessary to rub flour on the dough), and presses it into the dough. The cutter should not be pressed all the way through the dough, as that makes it difficult to remove. The child then lifts the cutter and removes the excess dough with a knife or stick. The cookie is ready to bake. Use the small brush to clean the dough from the cutter when necessary.

cookie with excess dough removed

pressing the cutter into the dough

Individual Educational Objectives

The coins are greatly enlarged on the cookies, and each coin has its name and a date on it. This activity helps the children practice money identification skills.

Big Coin Rubbings

Materials Needed

Money Coaster Kit (see Advance Preparations)
plain white paper, lightweight — 1 sheet for each child
clear tape
crayons
scissors
colored construction paper, 9″ × 12″ — 1 sheet for each
   child
paste

Advance Preparations

The Money Coaster Kit includes materials to make 36 three-inch coasters. There are templates for the five coins plus ones for two old coins, the Buffalo nickel and the Indian-head penny. Also included are copper and silver foil, wooden and felt bases, black paint, glue, and sticks to do the foil rubbings. Complete directions are included in the kit, and the children could make the coasters as well as use the templates to make the coin rubbings in this activity. The kit may be purchased in craft and hobby stores or ordered directly from S & S Arts and Crafts, Colchester, Connecticut 06415.

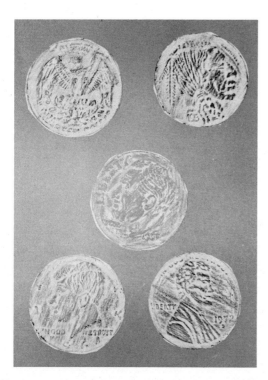

These rubbings were made by crayoning on paper placed over the templates. The rubbings were then cut out and pasted on construction paper.

The money coasters are made by rubbing foil with a stick.

34

Directions

Let each child choose a template with the coin picture of his or her choice and tape it to the underside of the sheet of white paper. Working on a desk, table, or other firm surface, the child crayons lightly back and forth across the part of the paper that is over the template. The entire template surface must be colored for the picture to "come up." The child may make rubbings of several coins using differently colored crayons. When all the rubbings are completed, the child cuts them out, arranges them on a sheet of construction paper, and pastes them in place.

Individual Educational Objectives

With these templates, all the coins are the same size. The child is challenged to identify the coins by the enlarged pictures only. Realistic pictures that resemble the ones on actual coins appear on the front and back of each template. Help the children identify the pictures. (Refer to *Introducing Coins and Bills*, pages 6-10, to verify the names of the people and things appearing on the real coins.) The child receives kinesthetic and tactile information when working with the raised pictures on the templates.

Real Coin Rubbings

Materials Needed

real penny, nickel, dime, quarter, and half dollar — 2 of each
tape
tracing paper or thin paper, 9″ × 12″ — 1 sheet for each child

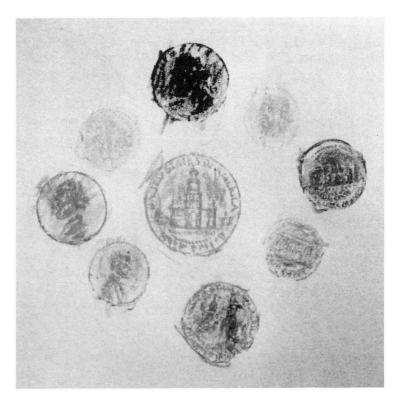

Stephanie made these rubbings using both heads and tails of a penny, nickel, dime, and quarter, and tails of a half dollar.

Directions

Tape each coin to the table or desk by putting a loop of tape, sticky side out, on the underside of the coin and pressing it to the table or desk surface. With the two coins of each denomination, tape one coin with heads up and the other with tails up.

The child puts the paper over a coin where he or she wants the image to be made and rubs a crayon gently over the coin. The coin's picture will show up. The child should not leave any uncrayoned spaces over the coin. The child may make as many rubbings on the paper as he or she wishes, with both heads and tails of each coin and with different coins in different colors.

Individual Educational Objectives

Kinesthetic and tactile skills are enhanced as the child feels the coins and watches their pictures develop on the paper. Very attractive designs may be made. The activity gives visual focus to the coin pictures and helps the children learn to recognize coins and distinguish between heads and tails of each coin. The smaller size of the coin rubbings in this activity compared to their larger size in the previous activity, and the size differences of the coins in this activity compared to the identical sizes in the previous activity, foster higher-level skills of coin recognition.

Lincoln and Washington Plates

Materials Needed

Lincoln penny and Washington quarter templates from the Money Coaster Kit (see previous activity)
several real pennies and quarters
masking tape
plain white paper, lightweight — 1 sheet for each child
brown or copper-colored crayons for penny rubbing — 1 for each child
black or gray crayons for quarter rubbing — 1 for each child
scissors
plain white paper plates, large size — 2 for each child
glue or paste

Katie designed this President Lincoln plate. She made three real penny rubbings and two big template rubbings, and decorated the plate with red and blue lines around the edge.

optional: red and blue pens or crayons; red, blue, and silver stars; patriotic stickers or ribbons; or other materials for decorating plates

Directions

Before the children decorate the plates, have them make the penny and quarter rubbings. Secure each template and real coin to a table or desk top by using a loop of masking tape with the sticky side out. Put the tape on the underside of the template or coin and press it to the work surface. Put plain white paper over the templates and coins, and tape the edges so the paper will not shift when the rubbing is done.

Have the child use a brown or copper-colored crayon for the penny rubbings and a black or gray crayon for the quarter rubbings. The child may crayon lightly over the paper until the features and designs on the templates and

coins show clearly. An effective way to crayon is to use the side of a ¾-inch long crayon. When the rubbing is completed, the pictures may be cut out.

Have each child glue the penny and quarter rubbings on separate plates. The plates may then be decorated in a patriotic motif by coloring with red and blue pens or crayons and by gluing on stars, ribbons, decorative stickers, or any other materials. The names "Lincoln" and "Washington" may be printed directly on the plates or on separate pieces of paper that are then stapled to the plates.

Individual Educational Objectives

Before beginning the activity, you may want to show pictures, read stories, or have a class discussion in order to better acquaint the children with the two Presidents whose birthdays are celebrated in February. This activity may coincide with Lincoln's birthday, February 12, and Washington's birthday, February 21. The children may gain a greater appreciation for these two holidays.

This activity helps emphasize identification of the penny and quarter. Tactile-kinesthetic awareness is fostered by the rubbings. Association skills, figure-ground skills, and eye-hand coordination are practiced, too.

Raul designed this President Washington plate. Along with the large template rubbing, he made four real quarter rubbings.

Coin Paperweights

John made these molds of a quarter, penny, nickel, and dime. By leaving the coin impressions unpainted on the quarter, penny, and dime molds, and painting only the coin impression on the penny mold, the size differences of the coins are obvious.

Materials Needed

real penny, nickel, dime, quarter, and half dollar — 1 of each
Vaseline, cooking oil, or liquid soap
small plastic cups (3½-ounce size) — 1 for each child
plaster of Paris
stick to stir plaster
straight pin or safety pin
poster paints or watercolor paints and brushes

Plaster of Paris

Mix the plaster in a container that can be discarded. (Do *not* pour or wash plaster down a sink drain. It will harden in the pipes.) Mix about one cup of plaster with about ¾ cup of water, and stir with the stick until the water is thoroughly absorbed. The mixture should be thick and creamy. This amount will make about four molds.

Directions

Let each child choose a coin that he or she would like to use for a mold. The child takes a tiny bit of Vaseline, oil, or soap, and rubs it all over both sides and the edges of the coin. Next, the child centers the coin in the bottom of the small cup. The coin side that faces up is the side that will show on the mold.

Mix the plaster according to the directions given above. Pour plaster mixture into each cup to a depth of about 1½ inches. The plaster will harden quickly. Allow about an hour for the mixture to harden and dry thoroughly. Then press the mold out of the cup. Pry the coin off the top with the end of a pin.

Let each child paint his or her mold. It is better to leave the coin impressions unpainted or to paint them a light color so the picture imprints can be seen easily. The finished molds may be used as decorative paperweights. After about a week, when the plaster and paint have dried thoroughly, a felt circle may be cut to size and glued to the base of each mold, and white glue may be brushed over the sides and the top surface to make a nice finish.

Individual Educational Objectives

This activity helps familiarize the children with the coins, their features, and their relative sizes. Individual coin size is emphasized by the molds, so size discrimination is practiced. The children can guess which coins will fit the molds by size. The real coins will fit neatly into the mold impressions. The children also might enjoy making prints in clay with the molds. Since the molds show reverse images of the coins, the clay prints will be realistic images. Help the children observe and identify the coin prints.

Coin Tracings

Materials Needed

real pennies, nickels, and dimes — 1 of each for each child
plain white or manila paper — 1 sheet for each child
pencils or pens
coin stamps such as Teaching Resources' *Coin Stamps:
  Heads and Tails* and ink pad

Directions

Have each child trace around his or her coins in random
order over the entire sheet of paper. When the tracings are
completed, have the children exchange papers and see if
they can correctly fill in each coin outline with the appropriate coin stamp picture.

Optional: If you have Teaching Resources' *Coins and Bills,*
the children can use the cards, with the coins pushed out of
them, as templates. These templates may be used either
instead of or in addition to the real coins.

Individual Educational Objectives

Only three coins are used in this activity so the children are
not overwhelmed with too many coins at one time. The
activity could be repeated at a later time using four or all
five coins. The activity gives the children experience in dis-
covering the relative sizes of the coins and in matching the
sizes with the appropriate coins. If you use real coins for
the tracing, the activity provides tactile experience.

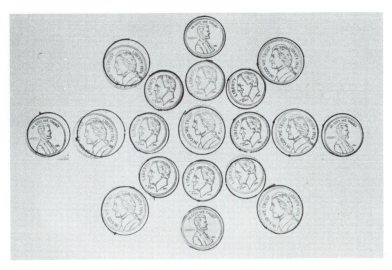

Stephanie made this coin design by first tracing around a penny,
nickel, and dime and then using coin stamps to print a picture of
each coin in the correct outline.

Hidden Money Picture

Materials Needed

real pennies, nickels, dimes, quarters, and half dollars —
    1 of each for each child (Several children could share a
    half dollar.)
plain white paper, 9" × 12" — 1 sheet for each child
colored felt-tipped marking pens *or* pen for tracing around
    the coins and crayons for coloring

Ross drew this picture using colored pens. He made several fig-
ures in the picture by drawing around each of the five coins.
Below the picture, he wrote questions asking how many of each
coin you can find in the picture.

Directions

Have each child draw a picture with the different sized coin
circles hidden in it. You may want to make a list of things
that are circular in shape, such as apples, oranges, grape-
fruit, balls, wheels, rings, hoops, circle faces, dishes, lids,
bowls, clocks, trays, saucers, holes, and doughnuts. If some
children cannot think of ideas for their pictures, suggest
that they draw a money tree and hide the coins among the
branches or hang them from the tree like apples. When the
pictures are completed, everyone can guess where the coin
circles are in each other's pictures and name the coin that
might fit each circle.

Individual Educational Objectives

This activity provides practice in discriminating the relative
sizes of coins and in figure-ground discrimination. Imagina-
tion and creativity are stimulated, and the activity is enjoyed by children who like art.

Coin Match

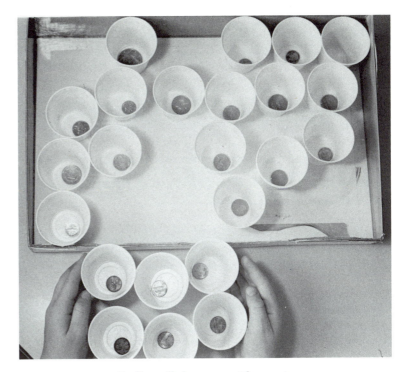

finding all the cups with pennies

Materials Needed

small plastic cups (3½-ounce size) — 20-40
real coins or facsimile coins such as coins from Teaching
    Resources' *Coins and Bills* — 1 for each cup (see
    Advance Preparations)
shallow box lid or tray to hold the cups

Advance Preparations

Put one coin in each cup. Suggested coins are: one half dollar, two quarters, and the remaining number divided evenly
among dimes, nickels, and pennies. Put the cups in the box
lid or on the tray in random order

Directions

Ask the child to find all the cups that have pennies in them,
remove the cups, and put them together in one place. When
the child has done this, ask the child to count the cups and
then ask, "How many pennies are there?" Follow this same
procedure in directing the child to find the other coins.

Individual Educational Objectives

This activity involves sorting, identifying, and grouping
coins and verbalizing the experience. This is a beginning
money activity that helps keep the child's interest and attention because of the necessity of looking into each cup.
Through curiosity, the child strengthens his or her visual
discrimination of the coins. The activity helps decrease dis-
tractions. If more than one child is participating, each child
is eager for a turn.

41

Coin Cubes

Materials Needed

coin cubes, teacher-made (see Advance Preparations) or
purchased (see Teaching Resources' *Money Cubes*)

Advance Preparations

Glue white paper to each face of two small wooden blocks.
Use coin stamps such as Teaching Resources' *Coin Stamps:
Heads and Tails* to print heads and tails of each coin on the
paper. Color the sixth face of each cube red to signify *stop*
or *lose your turn.* Or you may want to print *$1.00* on these
faces. Brush white glue liberally over each face of both
cubes. When the glue dries, it will be clear and will help
preserve the coin pictures. An alternate way to make the
coin cubes is to glue a facsimile coin to each face. (**Note:**
Teaching Resources' *Money Cubes* could be used for this
activity.)

Directions

One Cube: Use one cube for a coin identification game. Let
each child in turn toss the cube and then name the coin
shown on the top face. Games could be played in which the
child must not only name the coin but also state its value
both in words and in writing. For example, a child would
say, "penny," and "one cent," and write *1¢*.

Two Cubes: Use two cubes for addition and subtraction
activities. Each child in turn tosses two cubes and then adds
the values of the two coins shown on the cubes or subtracts
the smaller value from the higher one, depending on the
rule you establish at the start of the game. In this game, the
red face of each cube may count as zero.

Individual Educational Objectives

Activities with these coin cubes facilitate coin recognition
and value recall. Adding and subtracting coin values mentally and verbalizing the answer are other skills fostered.

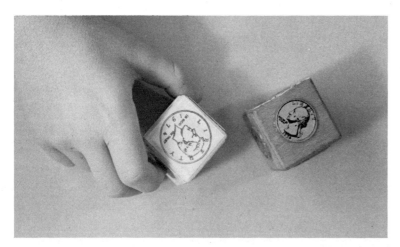

John is holding a cube with a coin stamp print on each face. The
other cube has a facsimile coin glued to each face.

Coin Feelies

Materials Needed

tube socks, as pictured, or other large socks — 5 (see Advance Preparations)
real pennies, nickels, dimes, quarters, and half dollars — 2 of each (see Advance Preparations)
optional: paper plate (see Advance Preparations)

With his right hand, Chris points to the coin he feels with his left hand in the sock.

Advance Preparations

You may decorate each sock with claws, with eyes, a nose, and a mouth to make a face, or with any other design or decoration that would add interest and appeal. Without letting the children see, put a different coin in each sock toe. Put the matching set of five coins out on the table or in a paper plate.

Directions

Each child in turn puts his or her hand into each sock and feels the coin without removing it. At the same time, the child feels the coins on the table with his or her other hand. The child tries to identify the coin in each sock. After he or she has named a coin, the child may take it out of the sock and look at it (without letting the other children see it) to verify his or her answer.

Individual Educational Objectives

This is a *very* beginning activity that can even be used with five-year-olds. The activity helps the children distinguish coins by tactile discrimination and is a fun way to practice coin identification skills. The activity reinforces the learning of coin names and discrimination of size differences.

Penny Rubbings in Patterns

Materials Needed

stencils of a circle, square, triangle, and rectangle (see Advance Preparations)
tracing paper or thin white paper, 9" × 12" — 1 sheet for each child
pens or pencils — 1 for each child
real pennies — 1 for each child
tape
crayons

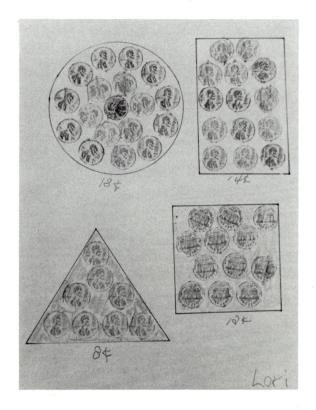

Advance Preparations

Make cardboard stencils of a circle, square, triangle, and rectangle for the children to trace. Patterns are provided on page 83.

Directions

Have each child first trace one or more of the basic-shape stencils on the sheet of paper. (With some children, you may want to prepare the sheet for them ahead of time.) Tape a penny to each child's work surface with a small loop of tape, sticky side out. The child puts the paper over the penny so the coin is inside one of the shapes. The child then crayons gently over the coin. When this rubbing is completed, the child moves the paper and makes another penny rubbing next to the first. This procedure is repeated until the entire shape is filled with penny rubbings. The child then counts the pennies and writes the amount below the shape. (You may need to write the amount for some children.)

Individual Educational Objectives

This activity helps increase the children's awareness of the pictures on the penny, so coin recognition is practiced. The activity helps the children become aware of the coin's size and how many will fit in a given space. Beginning counting skills are fostered. At a higher level, the same activity could be done with a nickel, dime, or quarter.

Fingertip Money

Materials Needed

plain white paper, 9" × 12" — 1 sheet for each child
marking pen
coin stamps such as Teaching Resources' *Coin Stamps: Heads and Tails* and ink pad
optional: real coins or facsimile coins such as coins from Teaching Resources' *Coins and Bills*

Directions

Have each child put both hands on the paper and spread his or her fingers apart. With the marking pen, trace around the child's hands.

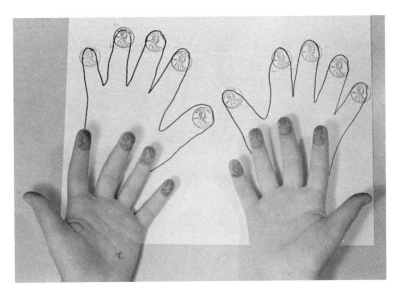

Pennies are stamped on each fingertip in the hand tracing. Dimes are stamped on David's left fingertips and pennies on his right fingertips.

Counting by Ones: Using the penny coin stamp or the real or facsimile pennies, the child puts one cent on each fingertip in the hand tracing. Each time the child adds a penny, ask, "How many cents are there now?" Next, use the penny stamp to stamp a penny picture on each of the child's fingertips. Play games asking the child to show you a certain number of cents: for example, "How many cents are on one hand?" and "How many cents are there on both hands?" Ask the child how many fingers are on one hand and on both hands. Let the children take turns giving each other directions such as, "Please show me ____ cents." The child given the direction must hold up the correct number of fingers.

Counting by Fives: Follow the same procedure given above, but use the nickel instead of the penny.

Counting by Tens: Use the dime instead of the penny.

Adding Coin Values: Print a dime on each fingertip of the child's left hand and a nickel or penny on each fingertip of his or her right hand. Ask the child to use his or her fingers to show you amounts that equal 45 cents, 51 cents, or other combinations. This is fascinating and challenging for the young gifted child.

Individual Educational Objectives

This activity lends itself to adaptations for different levels of learning. Counting by ones is a beginning-level task. Counting by fives or tens is a higher-level task. Adding different coin values is a challenging task. At all levels, the activity involves recognizing coins and verbalizing answers. The child's kinesthetic involvement enhances learning.

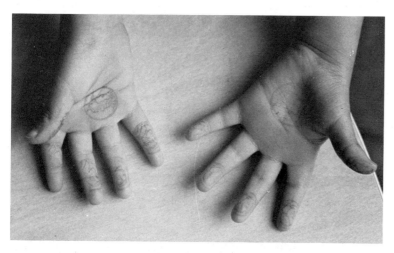

Gaston has a nickel stamped on each right fingertip and a quarter stamped in his right palm, to show that five nickels equal one quarter. He has a dime stamped on each left fingertip and a half dollar stamped in his left palm, to show that five dimes equal one half dollar.

Money Trays

Materials Needed

small, shallow containers such as aluminum pie pans or
    sturdy paper plates — 6 (see Advance Preparations)
real coins or facsimile coins such as coins from Teaching
    Resources' *Coins and Bills* (see Advance Preparations)
answer sheets — 1 for each child (see Advance Prepara-
    tions)
pens or pencils — 1 for each child

Advance Preparations

Put two or more coins in each container according to the
children's ability to identify them and add their values.
Number six small cards from one to six in large numerals,
and put a card in each container. Prepare an answer sheet
for each child. (You may make the sheet on a spirit master
and run off multiple copies.) Write *Name* at the top of the
sheet with a line for the child to write in his or her name,
and number from one to six in a column with a line next to
each numeral, for the child to write in his or her answers.

Directions

Give each child an answer sheet. Pass out the numbered
containers, one to each child. It does not matter in which
order a child gets each container. (If there are more than six
children participating, some children will have to wait a
turn.) Each child looks at the coins in his or her container,
adds their values, and writes the answer next to that number on the answer sheet. For example, if a child has container #4 and it has two dimes in it, the child would write
20¢ next to numeral 4 on his or her answer sheet. The children should keep passing the containers around and ask for
the ones they need in order to complete the answer sheet.
When each child has seen all six containers, check the
children's answers as a group. Let them use crayons to correct their own papers. When checking, start with container
#1 and ask a child to name the coins in that container, iden-
tify each coin's value, and state the total value of coins in
the container.

Individual Educational Objectives

This activity helps develop skills of coin recognition and
addition. It may be used frequently, with adaptations for
different levels of money skills. At a very beginning level,
you may limit the activity to simple coin recognition by
putting only one coin in each container. Later, two identical
coins may be combined in each container. For beginners,
you may want to put all pennies in the containers, a different number in each container. Later, the nickel can be
added. Nickels and pennies can predominate for a while,
and then add dimes. Another time, add a penny to a single
coin in each container. Later, add a dime to a single
coin in each container. As the children's skill increases, add a dollar

to the coin in each container. Keep repeating combinations until all of the children get correct answers. Increase the number of coins and the difficulty of the combinations as the children's skills become more advanced. Important combinations are: five pennies; two nickels; two to five dimes; two quarters; and two half dollars. Using several nickels or dimes in each container provides practice in counting by fives or tens. Beginning children may write the answers with cent marks. More advanced children can write answers using the decimal point and dollar sign.

Animal Banks

Materials Needed

large animal banks (dinosaur, whale, pig, turtle) — 1 of each for each child (see Advance Preparations)
real coins or facsimile coins such as coins from Teaching Resources' *Coins and Bills* — 1 penny, nickel, dime, quarter, and half dollar for each child
pens or pencils — 1 for each child

Advance Preparations

Patterns for large animal banks are provided on pages 84-85. Make a copy of each bank for each child. The patterns include coin outlines within each bank. You may substitute other coin combinations in each bank to meet your students' needs.

Directions

Give each child the four animal banks and a set of five coins. The child fits the coins into the outlines on each bank and then writes the coin values within the outlines. Tell the child to make sure the outline circle is close to the edge of the actual coin being fitted to the outline. When the child has identified all the coins, he or she may color the bank, leaving the coin circles uncolored.

Individual Educational Objectives

Fitting the coins to the outlines gives the children practice in identifying the coins and in discriminating their relative sizes. Handling the coins gives them tactile information about coin size. With more advanced children, have the children total the amount of money in each bank.

Put Money in the Bank

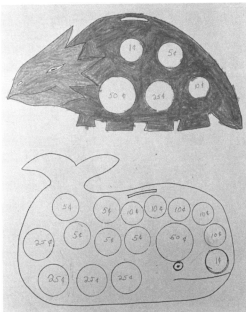

The coins in these banks have been correctly identified by Ross. These pictures may be used to check your students' answers.

Materials Needed

small animal banks (pig, rabbit, turtle, duck) — 1 of each
    for each child (see Advance Preparations)
coin stamps such as Teaching Resources' *Coin Stamps:
    Heads and Tails* and ink pad *or* real coins *or* facsimile
    coins such as coins from Teaching Resources' *Coins and
    Bills*
optional: crayons for making coin rubbings

Advance Preparations

Patterns for small animal banks are provided on page 86. Make a copy of each bank for each child. If you feel that these banks will present too difficult an eye-hand coordination task for the children, use the large animal banks instead (patterns on pages 84-85).

Chris has made penny rubbings in each bank.

Directions

If you are working with an individual child, give the child the banks, the coin stamps, and an ink pad. If you are working with a small group of children, give each child the banks and a supply of real or facsimile coins.

Give each child directions for putting money in each bank, such as, "Put ten cents in the pig bank." If the child is using the coin stamps, he or she could, for this example, stamp a dime, two nickels, a nickel and five pennies, or ten pennies in the bank. If the child is using real or facsimile coins, he or she could position those coins in the bank. Vary your directions according to the child's ability and individual needs. For a more advanced child, for example, you could say, "Put thirty-five cents in the turtle bank," and "Put one dollar in coins in the duck bank."

As an alternate way of putting money in each bank, the child could make coin rubbings as shown in the picture.

Individual Educational Objectives

This activity is more difficult than the previous one, which also used animal banks, because in this activity the children must decide which coins to put in each bank rather than simply match coins to their outlines. Identification of coin values and addition skills are fostered. If you wish to make this a more independent activity, write an amount below each bank, and have the child draw around the coins he or she puts in each bank and then write the coin value in each outline. Check the children's work as a small-group activity.

How Much Is a Dime?

Materials Needed

plain white paper — 1 sheet for each child
real pennies, nickels, and dimes — 1 of each for each child
pens or pencils — 1 for each child
optional: coin stamps such as Teaching Resources' *Coin Stamps: Heads and Tails* and ink pad

Directions

Structure this activity by directing the child step-by-step. Tell the child to put the dime near the top-left corner of the paper and trace around it. (**Note:** If the child needs help in keeping the coin in place, put a loop of tape, sticky side out, on the underside of the dime and then press it to the paper.) Then have the child either write the coin value inside the outline or stamp the dime picture in the outline.

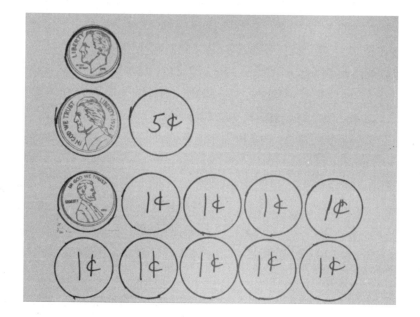

Next, tell the child to trace around two nickels side by side below the dime and then write in the coin value or print its picture. This illustrates that two nickels equal one dime. Finally, have the child trace around 10 pennies in two rows below the nickels and write in the coin value or stamp the coin picture. Have the child count the pennies to emphasize that 10 pennies equal two nickels or one dime.

Individual Educational Objectives

This structured activity clearly illustrates the different coins that equal 10 cents. Coin identification and values are practiced.

How Much Is a Quarter?

Materials Needed

plain white paper — 1 sheet for each child
real pennies and quarters — 1 of each for each child (Several children could share a quarter.)
pens or pencils — 1 for each child
optional: coin stamps such as Teaching Resources' *Coin Stamps: Heads and Tails* and ink pad

Directions

Tell the child to put the quarter in the center of the paper, trace around it, and then write *25¢* or stamp the quarter picture in the outline. Around this, in a random arrangement or in a planned design, the child should trace around a penny 25 times and then write *1¢* in each outline, or stamp the penny picture 25 times. The child should then draw lines connecting the pennies with the quarter.

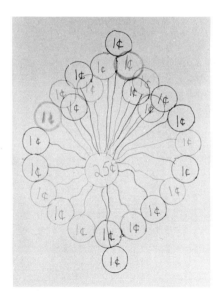

This design was made by tracing a penny 25 times.

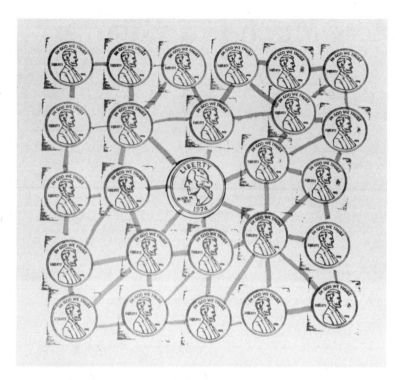

This design was made by stamping a penny 25 times.

Individual Educational Objectives

This activity fosters an understanding of the value of a quarter and reinforces, both visually and kinesthetically, the fact that 25 pennies equal one quarter.

How the Quarter Got Its Name

Materials Needed

plain white paper — 1 sheet for each child
real pennies, nickels, dimes, and quarters — 1 of each for each child (Several children could share a quarter.)
pens or pencils — 1 for each child
optional: coin stamps such as Teaching Resources' *Coin Stamps: Heads and Tails* and ink pad

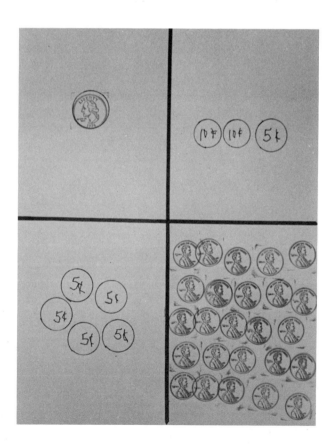

Directions

Demonstrate to the children how to fold the paper into quarters: fold the paper in half once, make a good crease by pressing with your fingers, fold it in half again, and crease. Open the paper to show the children the four quarters and explain that you have divided it into quarters, which means "fourths." Have each child fold his or her paper into quarters following your demonstration. The children can draw lines over the creases to emphasize the fourths.

Tell the children to trace around or stamp a quarter in the upper-left quarter. Tell them to trace around a dime twice or stamp two dimes in the upper-right quarter. Ask them how much money has to be added to the dimes to equal one quarter, and then have them trace around or stamp a nickel alongside the two dimes. Then tell them to trace around a nickel five times or stamp five nickels in the lower-left quarter. Finally, have them trace around a penny 25 times or stamp 25 pennies in the lower-right quarter.

When the project is finished, ask the children, "How much is one quarter?" "How much is two quarters?" "How much is three quarters?" and finally, "How much is four quarters?" An easier way to word this for some children is to say, "How much is a quarter and a quarter?" and point to the top two quarters on a sheet, then repeat the same question and point to the bottom two quarters on a sheet, and finally ask, "How much is fifty cents and fifty cents?" By this time the children will realize how the quarter got its name.

Individual Educational Objectives

This activity fosters skills of size discrimination and coin recognition and helps develop an understanding of comparative coin values.

Floating Target

Materials Needed

plastic dishpan, about 12" × 14" × 6" deep (see Advance Preparations)
water (see Advance Preparations)
small, shallow, flat-bottomed container or lid, about 3" or 4" wide (see Advance Preparations)
real penny, nickel, dime, quarter, and half dollar — 1 of each
paper and pencil for recording scores

Advance Preparations

Fill the dishpan about half full of water, and float the small container.

Directions

Each child in turn tosses the five coins, one by one, trying to get them in the small container. You may have the child name each coin before he or she tosses it, or you may name the coin that the child is to toss. Any coins that land in the floating container are counted in the child's score. If the game is played many times, each child may keep a record of the number of coins of each denomination that landed in the floating container.

Individual Educational Objectives

Counting and identification of coins are skills practiced in this activity. This game is fun and can be used as a special treat or a special learning motivator. The coins may be varied. For example, if the children are just learning to count, use only pennies. If they are learning to count by fives, use only nickels.

Collect a Bundle

Materials Needed

game board (see Advance Preparations)
die
facsimile pennies, nickels, dimes, quarters, and half dollars, either teacher-made (see Advance Preparations) or purchased (such as coins from Teaching Resources' *Coins and Bills*)
large container for game "bank"
small containers — 1 for each player
place markers such as plastic chips or small pieces of colored paper — 1 differently colored marker for each child

Advance Preparations

A game board is provided on page 87. This board includes all five coins. If the children are less advanced, you could make a simpler game board showing only pennies and nickels or any other combination. You also might want to make a board showing both heads and tails of the coins. The coin pictures can be printed with stamps such as Teaching Resources' *Coin Stamps: Heads and Tails.*

You will need an ample supply of facsimile coins for this activity. If you do not purchase the coins, you could use coin stamps to print them on small squares of paper. If your class is using printed money in a classroom economy, print this game money on differently colored paper to distinguish it from the other money. The game begins with all the money in the "bank" container.

Directions

The game may be played by two to eight players. You may want to make several copies of the game board and let the children play in pairs. The players begin in the START space, move across the top as shown by the arrow, and continue around until they reach the STOP space. Each child in turn tosses the die and then moves his or her marker the number of spaces shown on the die. The player names the coin in the space in which he or she landed, takes that coin from the "bank," and puts it in his or her own container. When all the players have reached STOP, each player counts the money in his or her container. The player with the most money is the winner.

The children may want to go around the game board several times instead of only once. The number of times could be agreed upon before the game starts. An alternate method is to set a timer for a given length of time. When the timer rings, the players stop and count their money.

Individual Educational Objectives

This game reinforces coin identification skills and counting. Reinforce the learning process by letting each child identify the coin in each turn and collect the correct coin from the "bank" by himself or herself. The game could be played by beginners as a coin identification game only: instead of adding up the total amount of money he or she has collected, each player could simply count the number of each coin.

To extend the game and provide a greater challenge, have each player describe something associated with the coin on which he or she lands in each turn. For example, the child could say, "It's my birthday and I got fifty cents," for a half dollar; "It's my allowance," for a quarter; "It's a present from my aunt," for a dime; "I earned it for good school work," for a nickel; and "I found this lucky penny," for a penny. Encourage each child to think of associations on his or her own.

Ball Toss

Materials Needed

one 36-cup egg separator or three 12-cup egg cartons (see Advance Preparations)
box with low sides to fit the separator or egg cartons (see Advance Preparations)
small self-sticking labels — 36 (see Advance Preparations)
marking pen (see Advance Preparations)
optional: coin stamps such as Teaching Resources' *Coin Stamps: Heads and Tails* and ink pad (see Advance Preparations)
facsimile coins such as coins from Teaching Resources' *Coins and Bills* (see Advance Preparations)
Ping Pong ball or other small, lightweight ball

Advance Preparations

Put the separator or cartons in a box with low sides. (The box keeps the ball from bouncing away when it hits the separator or cartons.) With the marking pen, print 1¢, 5¢, 10¢, 25¢, and 50¢ on the labels. For variety, you may want to print coin pictures on some labels. Put one label in each cup of the separator or cartons, positioning the labels so they all can be read from one side of the box. Put the facsimile coins in a box, for use as a "bank" in keeping score. Or, if you wish, you could simply keep score with pencil and paper.

As an alternate method, you could put from one to three coins in each egg cup — pennies in the 1¢ cup, nickels in the 5¢ cup, and so forth. This may be done as a sorting task for the children before they start the game. When the tossed ball lands in a cup, the child takes a coin. When all the coins in a cup are gone, a score of zero would occur if the ball lands in that cup.

Directions

Have a child stand a foot or more away from the box and toss the ball. When it lands in a cup, the child lifts it out and reads the amount or identifies the value of the coin shown on the label. The child takes a coin of that value from the "bank." If you have put coins in the cups, the child takes one from the cup in which the ball landed. The next child then takes a turn. Continue until all the children have had a predetermined number of turns or, if you put coins in the cups, until all the cups are empty. The children's scores may be kept by letting them collect coins and then counting them or by writing down each child's score in each turn and then totaling the amounts.

Individual Educational Objectives

This activity involves reading coin values and recognizing coin pictures and the coins themselves. Adding scores, sorting, and counting money are additional skills practiced.

Coin Toss

Materials Needed

coin target (see Advance Preparations)
real penny
pencil and paper for keeping score

Advance Preparations

A coin target is provided on page 89. Make a copy of that target, or make your own by printing (or having a child print) many pictures of the five coins on a sheet of paper.

Directions

Put the coin target flat on a table or on the floor. Each child in turn tosses a penny onto the target. Have the child name the coin or coins the penny landed on. Keep a record of the number and name of the coin or coins touched. After a set number of turns, add the amounts for each child.

Individual Educational Objectives

This activity helps develop the ability to recognize and name coins. More capable children could keep track of their own scores. In this case, counting and addition skills are also practiced.

Egg Box Shake

Materials Needed

egg carton, one dozen size (see Advance Preparations)
facsimile coins such as coins from Teaching Resources'
    Coins and Bills, or coin stamps such as Teaching
    Resources' *Coin Stamps: Heads and Tails,* ink pad,
    paper, and scissors
glue or tape (see Advance Preparations)
beads, ½" in diameter — 1 or 2 (see Advance Preparations)
pencil and paper for keeping score

Advance Preparations

Tape or glue a facsimile coin or a coin-stamped picture in
the bottom of each egg cup. You also may want to make a
coin identification chart on the lid, as shown in the photograph. For a coin identification game, put one bead in the

egg carton. For addition and subtraction games, put two
beads in the carton. (**Note:** You may want to prepare several cartons, each one using coins in different combinations,
according to the children's abilities and needs.)

Directions

Coin Identification Game: The child closes the carton and
shakes it. The child then opens the carton and looks to see
in which cup the bead landed, identifies the coin, and
records the amount on his or her paper. Let each child take
a specified number of turns.

Addition and Subtraction Games: The child shakes the carton, opens it, and names the coins in the cups in which the
two beads landed. The child records the amounts and the
sum (for example, 1¢ + 5¢ = 6¢). If both beads landed in
the same cup, the child should count the coin twice. For a
subtraction game, the child subtracts the value of the lower-
value coin from the higher-value one. If both beads landed
in the same cup, the child would count the coin twice (5¢ −
5¢, for example), and the answer would be zero.

Individual Educational Objectives

These games involve coin recognition and coin-value identification. When the children play with a carton containing
two beads, simple addition and subtraction skills and skills
of writing math symbols are practiced.

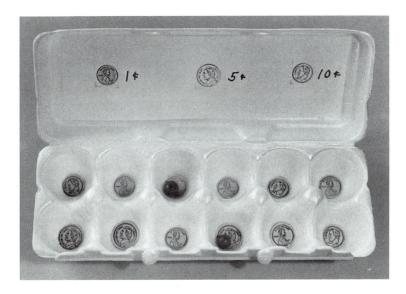

Add It Up

Materials Needed

egg cartons, one dozen size — 3 (see Advance Preparations)
scissors (see Advance Preparations)
marking pen (see Advance Preparations)
real coins or facsimile coins such as coins from Teaching
    Resources' *Coins and Bills*
paper squares — 12 (see Advance Preparations)
optional: lined paper — 1 sheet for each child
pencils or pens — 1 for each child

Advance Preparations

Cut each egg carton into four sections, each having three egg cups connected together in a straight line (see photograph). Mark a plus sign on each section between the first

and second cups, and mark an equal sign between the second and third cups. Put a coin in the first and second cups of each section. Cut 12 small squares from plain white paper. If you wish to do this activity with an individual child, leave the squares blank so the child can write in his or her answers. If you wish to work with a small group of children, number the squares from one to 12, and put a square in the third cup of each section.

Directions

Individual Activity: The child adds the values of the coins in the first and second cups of each section, writes the answer on a paper square, and puts the paper into the third cup. The child could do this independently and then check his or her answers with you after he or she has completed all 12 sections.

Small-Group Activity: Give each child a sheet of lined paper for recording his or her answers. Pass the numbered sections among the children. Each child adds the coin values as described above and writes the answer next to the number on his or her paper that corresponds to the number in the third cup of the section. When each child has seen all 12 sections, check the children's answers as a group activity.

Individual Educational Objectives

This activity fosters coin recognition, understanding and recording coin values and math symbols, and simple addition skills.

Coin-Picture Problems

Materials Needed

file cards, 3″ × 5″ — 10 (see Advance Preparations)
coin stamps such as Teaching Resources' *Coin Stamps: Heads and Tails* and ink pad (see Advance Preparations)
marking pen (see Advance Preparations)
paper squares, 10, or lined paper, 1 sheet for each child (see Advance Preparations)
real coins or facsimile coins such as coins from Teaching Resources' *Coins and Bills*
box to hold coins
pencils or pens — 1 for each child

Advance Preparations

On each file card, write an addition or subtraction problem by printing coin pictures, writing a plus or minus sign and an equal sign, and drawing an answer box (see photograph). If you do not have coin stamps, you could trace around real coins to make coin outlines. If you wish to do this activity with an individual child, leave the answer boxes blank and cut 10 small squares from plain white paper. If you wish to work with a small group of children, number the answer boxes from one to 10.

Directions

Individual Activity: For each card, the child selects real or facsimile coins from the box to match the ones printed on the card and puts them over the printed pictures. The child then writes the answer to the problem on a paper square and puts it over the answer box on the card. The child could do this independently and then check his or her work with you after he or she has completed all 10 cards.

Small-Group Activity: Give each child a sheet of lined paper for recording his or her answers. Pass the cards among the children. Each child matches real or facsimile coins to the pictures, as described above, and then writes the answers on his or her paper. When each child has seen all 10 cards, check the children's answers as a group activity.

Individual Educational Objectives

This activity helps the children learn to discriminate among coin pictures, match them with real or facsimile coins, and add and subtract coin values.

Egg Box Match

Materials Needed

egg cartons, one dozen size — several (see Advance
   Preparations)
scissors (see Advance Preparations)
marking pen (see Advance Preparations)
real coins or facsimile coins such as coins from Teaching
   Resources' *Coins and Bills*
box to hold coins

Advance Preparations

Cut the lid and flap off each egg carton. In each egg cup,
on the *outer* wall as shown in the photograph, write an
amount of money. The amounts may be chosen at random,

or you may show a progression such as 2¢, 4¢, 6¢, 8¢, 10¢;
or 5¢, 10¢, 15¢, 20¢, 25¢; or 4¢, 14¢, 24¢, 34¢, 44¢. By
writing the amount on the outer wall of each row of cups,
only one set of amounts is visible to the child at one time.
He or she must turn the carton around to see the amounts
in the other row.

Directions

Using real coins or facsimile coins from the box, the child
fills each egg cup with coins that equal the amount written
on that cup. Let the child select the coin combination he or
she wishes to use. For example, for 18¢, the child could put
in 18 pennies; three nickels and three pennies; a dime, a
nickel, and three pennies; two nickels and eight pennies; or
a dime and eight pennies.

Individual Educational Objectives

Reading and interpreting money symbols, recognizing and
comprehending money values, and mental math computa-
tions are skills fostered by this activity. After the child has
completed all 12 cups in a carton, you could ask the child
to show you other coin combinations that equal the amount
in each cup.

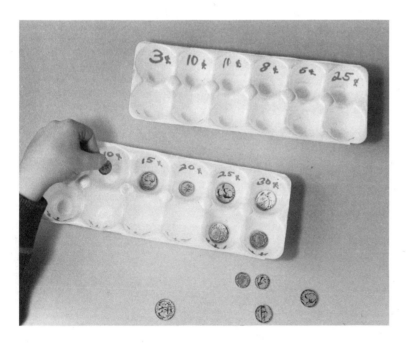

Fill to Order

Materials Needed

small cans such as juice cans — 10-15 (see Advance
    Preparations)
file cards, 3" × 5" — 5-8 (see Advance Preparations)
scissors (see Advance Preparations)
marking pen (see Advance Preparations)
box to hold cans (see Advance Preparations)
facsimile coins such as coins from Teaching Resources'
    Coins and Bills
box to hold coins

Advance Preparations

Cut the file cards in half lengthwise. Write an "order" (an
addition or subtraction problem) on each card and put it in
a can. Adjust the "orders" to meet the needs of the children
participating. The difficulty of the "orders" may be
increased as they progress. Put all the cans in the box.

Directions

The child puts coins in each can according to the "order"
written on the card. If the order is 4¢ + 10¢ = 14¢, the
child must put four pennies and a dime in the can. If the
order is 10¢ + 10¢ + 5¢ = 25¢, the child may put either
two dimes and a nickel or a quarter in the can.

Individual Educational Objectives

This activity involves recognizing coins, identifying coin
values, making decisions, and following directions. The
child must analyze each order, associate the written
amounts with coin values, and make a choice regarding
which coins to put in the can.

Ten Cents Plus and One Dollar Plus

Materials Needed

small white envelopes, about 4" × 6" — 6 (see Advance
   Preparations)
scissors (see Advance Preparations)
marking pen (see Advance Preparations)
real coins or facsimile coins such as coins from Teaching
   Resources' *Coins and Bills* (see Advance Preparations)
lined paper — 1 sheet for each child
pencils or pens — 1 for each child

Advance Preparations

Seal the envelopes and then cut each one in half to make
two pockets. On the outside of each of six pockets, write
10¢ plus. Number these pockets from one to six. On the
outside of each of the remaining six pockets, write *$1.00
plus.* Number these pockets from seven to 12. Put one or
more coins in each pocket.

Directions

Give each child a sheet of lined paper, and have the children number their papers from one to 12. Pass the 12 pockets among the children. Each child reads the notation on the
outside of each pocket, looks inside to identify the coin or
coins inside, and then writes the example and the answer on
his or her paper (for example, *10¢ + 5¢ = 15¢* or *$1.00 +
25¢ = $1.25*).

Individual Educational Objectives

This activity helps develop the skill of adding 10 or 100 to
any number. The activity involves recognizing coins, identifying coin values, and adding zero to a given number.

Money Envelopes

Materials Needed

medium-sized white envelopes — 5 (see Advance Preparations)
marking pen (see Advance Preparations)
real coins or facsimile coins such as coins from Teaching Resources' *Coins and Bills* (see Advance Preparations)
lined paper — 1 sheet for each child
pencils or pens — 1 for each child

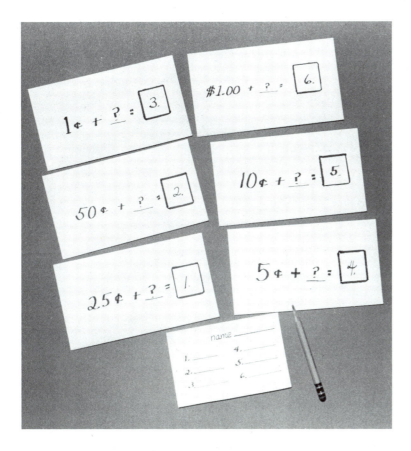

Advance Preparations

On the front of each envelope, write an addition or subtraction problem that includes an amount of money, a plus or minus sign, a question mark to indicate an amount of money you will place in the envelope, an equal sign, and an answer box (see photograph). Number the envelopes from one to five by writing the numerals in the answer boxes. Put one or more coins in each envelope. The problems should fit the children's current needs. Some examples are:

$2¢ + ? = $ _____ (Put a dime in the envelope; the answer is 12¢.)

$15¢ - ? = $ _____ (Put a nickel in the envelope; the answer is 10¢.)

$10¢ + ? = $ _____ (Put two nickels in the envelope; the answer is 20¢.)

Directions

Give each child a sheet of lined paper, and have the children number their papers from one to five. Pass the envelopes among the children. Each child reads the problem on the front of each envelope, looks inside it to see how much money the question mark represents, calculates the answer, and writes the answer next to the appropriate number on his or her paper.

Individual Educational Objectives

This activity helps the children learn to recognize coins, identify coin values, interpret math symbols, add and subtract coin amounts, and follow directions in sequence. Hiding the coins in the envelopes adds suspense and heightens interest. The envelopes may be reused for other problems; simply change the coins placed inside them to create new problems.

Dollar Build-Up

Materials Needed

file cards, 3" × 5" — 5 or more (see Advance Preparations)
marking pen (see Advance Preparations)
facsimile coins such as coins from Teaching Resources'
  Coins and Bills — at least one dollar's worth of each coin
container to hold coins

Advance Preparations

Write *$1.00* on each card. If you wish, you could use fac-
simile one-dollar bills instead of the cards.

Directions

Tell the child to group identical coins on each card so they
add up to one dollar. When counting the coins, the child
should start with the largest denomination and work down.

Encourage the child to look for half dollars first, group
them together, count out the number needed to equal one
dollar, and put those on the card. You might ask, "How
many make a dollar?" Next ask the child to look for quarters, group them, count out a dollar's worth, and put them
on another card. Continue through the dimes, nickels, and
pennies. When the child has completed a card for each coin
denomination, he or she could count the extra coins as
well.

Individual Educational Objectives

This activity involves sorting coins, counting money, and
using mental arithmetic. The marked cards help the child
organize the activity and keep the objective in mind.
Remind the child to look for the largest denomination first.
With some children, it might be helpful to have them sort
all the coins into piles of half dollars, quarters, dimes, nickels, and pennies before they count any out and put them on
cards.

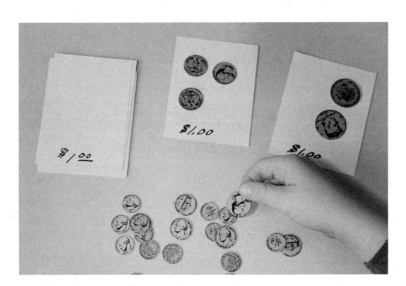

Money Make-a-Word

Materials Needed

small paper plates (see Advance Preparations)
wide felt marking pen (see Advance Preparations)
masking tape or string

Advance Preparations

Choose words you want to use for the activity, such as *penny, nickel, dime, quarter, dollar, money, coin, one, five, ten, bank,* or any others you wish to use. Print one letter on the back of each paper plate. Letter enough plates so you can spell each of the words you have chosen. You may attach a length of string to each plate by tying the ends through two holes punched near the top edge. The plate can then be hung from a child's neck.

Directions

Think of one of the money words and then choose plates with those letters. Tell the children how many letters are in the word, and ask for that number of volunteers. Hang a plate around each child's neck, or tape a plate to his or her chest using a loop of masking tape with the sticky side out. Give the volunteers a clue such as, "This is the name of a coin." Let the volunteers figure out the word and arrange themselves in order in a line to spell it. Let the rest of the children watch and monitor for errors. If the volunteers cannot figure out the word from your first clue, give another one — for example, "This coin is worth the same amount of money as two nickels."

Individual Educational Objectives

This gross-motor activity gives practice in spelling and problem-solving. It is an active and enjoyable game that helps reinforce the learning of money vocabulary.

Ross, Stephanie, Heather, and Christy line up to spell "dime."

Money Word Puzzles

Materials Needed ·

paper strips — 5 for each child (see Advance Preparations)
scissors (see Advance Preparations)
crayons
coin stamps such as Teaching Resources' *Coin Stamps: Heads and Tails* and ink pads (Several children can share each pad.)

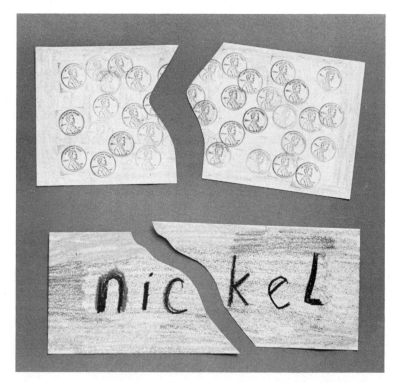

The penny puzzle (top) shows penny pictures made with a coin stamp. The word "penny" is printed on the other side. The nickel puzzle (bottom) shows the word printed on one side. Nickel pictures are stamped on the **other** side.

Advance Preparations

Before beginning the activity, you or the children should cut nine-inch by 12-inch sheets of white construction paper into strips measuring four inches by nine inches. With a crayon, print the name of a coin in large letters on one side of each strip. Make a set of five strips for each child: penny, nickel, dime, quarter, and half dollar.

Directions

Give each child a set of five strips. Suggest that they color or make designs on the coin-word side of each strip. On the other side, each child prints pictures of heads and tails of the coin named on the front. This side also may be colored and decorated. When each child has completed his or her five strips, you or the child should cut each strip in half to make a puzzle. Use irregular cuts rather than straight vertical cuts, so the puzzles will be self-correcting (see photograph).

Optional: On an extra strip, have the child print *$1.00* in large numerals and symbols. To give additional practice in making the dollar sign, have the child cover the reverse side of the strip with dollar signs.

Individual Educational Objectives

This activity reinforces knowledge of coin names and their pictures. Coin and word recognition skills are fostered. Encourage the children to color the entire surface of the word side and to print lots of coin pictures on the coin side. Explain that this will make a more interesting puzzle. More capable children could print the coin names themselves.

Money Word Signs

Materials Needed

letters that spell *penny, nickel, dime, quarter,* and *half dollar* (see Advance Preparations)
scissors (see Advance Preparations)
colored construction paper (pre-cutting optional, see Advance Preparations)
glue or paste

Advance Preparations

Pre-cut single letters from magazines, newspapers, cereal boxes, posters, and other sources. The letters should be from one half inch to three inches in height. Finding and cutting out the letters may be a project that includes all the children. If you wish, the colored paper may be pre-cut into 2½-inch by six-inch strips, or the paper may be cut after the child has selected letters and arranged them on the paper.

Directions

Write the coin names on the chalkboard or in some other prominent place so all the children can see them. Have each child choose letters to spell the words, making one or more words at a time, and arrange each set of letters on a sheet of colored paper. When the child has decided on a pleasing combination of letter sizes and forms, he or she may glue or paste the letters on the paper. If you are not using pre-cut strips, trim (or have the child trim) the sheet to an appropriate size.

Individual Educational Objectives

Reading and spelling skills are practiced in this activity. The child spells each word by concentrating on one letter at a time until the entire word is spelled. This emphasizes parts-to-whole relationships and sequencing skills. You or the children could sort the letters before beginning the signs so all A's are in one pile, all C's in another, and so forth. This simplifies the selection process. The spelling activity is enjoyable, and the completed signs are attractive. They may be used in various ways: to show prices in a class store, to show how much a child may earn for completing a task in a classroom economy, or simply as decorative signs.

Money Word Mix-Ups

Materials Needed

word list (see Advance Preparations)
lined paper — 1 sheet for each child
pencils or pens — 1 for each child

Advance Preparations

Make a list of money-related words that are appropriate for your students' reading, spelling, and vocabulary level. The list may include:

penny	count	money
nickel	change	buy
dime	heads	sell
quarter	tails	auction
half dollar	bank	rent
dollar	banker	jobs
one cent	teller	coins
five cents	earn	salary
ten cents	spend	store
twenty-five cents	save	advertise
fifty cents	payment	check
one dollar	price	deposit

Mixed-Up Words: Choose about five words from your list, and write them in large letters on paper or on the chalkboard so all the children can see them. On another sheet of paper or another area of the chalkboard, write one of the words with the letters scrambled — for example, *medi* for *dime*. Call on one of the children to come up and write the word with the correct spelling. Continue with other words. The children also could take turns choosing words and scrambling the letters.

Find the Word: Choose about five words and write them for all the children to see. You or a child chosen to be the leader should choose a word without telling the rest of the children what it is and draw a line for each letter in the word (for example, __ __ __ __ for *dime*). The other children try to guess the word by asking if it has specific letters in it. As soon as a child thinks he or she knows the word, the child may identify it. If the child is correct, he or she gets a point. If you are working with a large group of children, each child could write the word on paper as soon as the child thinks he or she knows what it is. All the children who guessed the word correctly get a point.

Vocabulary Game: Choose words that are not names of coins or coin values (for example, "save" and "auction"), and write them for all to see. The children earn points by defining each word and then using it in a sentence.

Individual Educational Objectives

Spelling and word comprehension skills are practiced in this activity. The difficulty of the activity can be controlled through the words you choose.

Money Sorting

Materials Needed

small jars or other containers — 15 (see Advance
    Preparations)
small self-sticking labels — 15 (see Advance Preparations)
marking pen (see Advance Preparations)
real coins or facsimile coins such as coins from Teaching
    Resources' *Coins and Bills*
box to hold coins

Advance Preparations

Label one set of five containers with the words *penny,
nickel, dime, quarter,* and *half dollar.* Label a second set
with the words *one cent, five cents, ten cents, twenty-five
cents,* and *fifty cents.* Label the third set with the amounts
1¢, 5¢, 10¢, 25¢, and 50¢.

Directions

Use one set of five containers, and arrange them in sequen-
tial order in front of the child. (If you wish, the child could
arrange them himself or herself.) Have the child sort coins
into the containers.

Individual Educational Objectives

Sorting coins reinforces identification skills and is a necessity in developing money-counting skills. Working with the
three sets of containers over a period of time helps the child
become familiar with the different ways that are used to
identify coins: coin names, coin values in words, and coin
values in symbols.

Money Match-Up

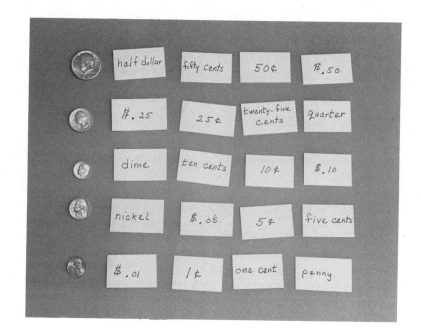

Materials Needed

cards with coin names and values — 1 set for each child
   (see Advance Preparations)
real coins or facsimile coins such as coins from Teaching
   Resources' *Coins and Bills* — 1 penny, nickel, dime,
   quarter, and half dollar for each child

Advance Preparations

To make each set of cards, cut five three-by-five file cards
into quarters to make 20 small cards measuring 1½ by 2½
inches. On these small cards, print coin names, coin values
in words, coin values in numerals with a cent sign, and coin
values in numerals with a dollar sign and decimal point (see
photograph).

Directions

Individual Activity: Give the child the five coins and a set
of cards. Have the child arrange the coins in decreasing
order in a vertical row (the half dollar at the top, the penny
at the bottom). Shuffle the cards and put them face down in
a stack. The child turns over each card, reads it, and puts it
next to the appropriate coin.

Small-Group Activity: In addition to the small cards, make
a set of large cards for use as call cards. Give each child the
five coins and a set of small cards. Have the children
arrange their coins as described above. Then have them sort
their small cards into the four types (coin names, coin
values in words, and so forth). Show the large cards one by
one. Each child looks through his or her small cards to find
the one that matches the large card and then puts it next to
the appropriate coin.

Small-Group Bingo Game: Give each child the five coins
and a set of small cards, and have them arrange their coins
as described above. Each child then shuffles his or her cards
and puts them face down in a stack. The child turns over
each card, reads it, and puts it next to the appropriate coin.
The first child who places all four cards for any one coin
calls "Bingo" and is the winner.

Individual Educational Objectives

This activity provides practice in coin recognition and coin-
value identification and helps the children learn the different ways in which coins can be identified. With more capable children, you may specify that they arrange the small
cards in a given order: coin names in the first column after
the actual coins, coin values in words in the second column, coin values in numerals with a cent sign in the third
column, and coin values in numerals with a dollar sign and
decimal point in the fourth column. (For additional materials that involve matching coins, coin names, and coin
values stated in different ways, see Teaching Resources'
Money Bingo.)

Point to the Coin

Materials Needed

instruction cards (see Advance Preparations)
real coins — 1 penny, nickel, dime, quarter, and half dollar
optional: tape recorder (see Advance Preparations), coin
stamps such as Teaching Resources' *Coin Stamps: Heads
and Tails*, ink pad, and a sheet of lined paper

Advance Preparations

Cut out the instruction cards provided on page 91. For
durability, cover the sheet with clear contact paper before
you cut out the cards. If you wish, you could make up your
own instructions and print them on small cards. If the children cannot read the instructions on their own and you
want to make this an independent activity, record the
instructions on a tape cassette.

Directions

Individual Activity: Arrange the five coins in order on the
table. Shuffle the cards and put them face down in a stack.
Turn over each card and read the instruction. (If the child is
capable of reading the instructions, have the child do so.)
The child responds to each instruction by pointing to and
naming the appropriate coin.

Small-Group Activity: Follow the same procedure described
above. Have the children take turns responding to the
instructions.

Independent Activity: Use the prerecorded tape cassette.
Give the child a set of coin stamps, an ink pad, and a sheet
of paper numbered to correspond to the numbered instructions. (Leave enough space between lines so the child can

stamp the coin pictures.) The child listens to each instruction, turns off the cassette player, and then stamps the
appropriate coin picture next to that number on the paper.

Individual Educational Objectives

This activity is an enjoyable way to test coin recognition
and coin-value identification. Either the individual activity
or the independent activity may be used for pre-testing or
post-testing; the small-group activity may be used for general evaluation. The instruction cards on page 91 are numbered for your convenience in recording a child's responses.
Incorrect responses indicate the coins or concepts with
which a child needs further work.

Shopping Lists

The jar marked $11.50 contained multivitamins.

Materials Needed

empty containers with prices marked on them (see Advance
  Preparations)
lined paper — 1 sheet for each child
pencils or pens — 1 for each child

Advance Preparations

Well in advance of this activity, ask the children to bring in
empty boxes, bottles, jars, cans, and other containers that
have prices marked on them. These might be toothpaste
boxes; jelly jars; cereal boxes; detergent boxes; spice bottles; vegetable, fruit, and juice cans; baby food jars; nut
cans; or any other containers.

Directions

Group several containers together on a desk or table. Each
child locates the price on each item, writes the price on his
or her paper, and finally adds the prices to find the total
price of that set of items. Other sets of items could be
placed in other locations. The children could take turns
itemizing and totaling the prices in each set.

Individual Educational Objectives

Locating and reading prices, writing them in a column to be
added, and comparing values are skills developed in this
activity. The children may also note the most expensive
item and the least expensive item in each set. You may want
to have them record the prices for each set in ascending or
descending order.

Searching the Ads

Materials Needed

two identical pages from newspaper advertising sections or
    from mail-order catalogs (see Advance Preparations)
scissors (see Advance Preparations)
plain paper, 9″ × 12″ — 1 sheet (see Advance Preparations)
tape or glue (see Advance Preparations)
scissors or marking pen for child

Advance Preparations

Cut out pictures of items advertised for sale on a newspaper
or catalog page. Do *not* cut out the prices. Tape or glue the
pictures to the paper.

Directions

Give the child the paper with the pictures and the second
copy of the original page. The child looks for each item on
the uncut page and either cuts out the price and tapes or
glues it to the paper, or writes the price on the paper below
each item.

Individual Educational Objectives

This activity helps the children become familiar with adver-
tisements. Searching the page for given items involves
figure-ground discrimination and matching skills.

How Much?

Materials Needed

newspaper advertising sections (see Advance Preparations)
scissors (see Advance Preparations)
masking tape (see Advance Preparations)
optional: large sheet of construction paper and crayons or
  colored marking pens (see Advance Preparations)
paper for calculating answers — 1 or more sheets for each
  child
pencils or pens — 1 for each child

Advance Preparations

As a preliminary activity, have the children cut prices from
newspaper ads. Encourage them to cut out the largest-sized
prices they can find. Using loops of masking tape with the
sticky side out, tape the prices to the chalkboard or a large
sheet of paper. The children could first draw a picture on
the paper, as shown in the photograph.

Directions

Make up addition problems whose sums will fit the prices
on display. For example, if one of the prices were $8.00,
you could say, "A bat costs five dollars, and a ball costs
three dollars. How much does the set cost?" Wait until all
of the children have figured out the answer and raised their
hands. Then call on one child to give the answer. If the
child is correct, let him or her take the price. Continue until
all the prices are gone.

Individual Educational Objectives

Cutting out the prices from the ads helps the children learn
to read prices as they are commonly stated in "real-life" situations. The children will discover that many items are

To make this poster, the children first drew a picture of a balloon
and then arranged the prices on it in order, with the highest prices
at the top and the lowest at the bottom.

priced in uneven dollar amounts — 33¢ or $5.99, for exam-
ple. Calculating the prices for the problems you state gives
the children practice in adding amounts of money. Adjust
the problems to the children's ability level. For example, if
the total price you wanted them to calculate were $3.98,
you could use $3.00 and 98¢ in the problem for beginning
children; $3.29 and 69¢ for more capable children; and 49¢,
$1.89, and $1.60 for more advanced children.

Which Would You Buy?

Materials Needed

magazine, catalog, or newpaper ads for toys, radios,
    albums, sports equipment, and other appealing items (see
    Advance Preparations)
scissors (see Advance Preparations)
white or colored construction paper, 9" × 12" (see
    Advance Preparations)
glue or tape (see Advance Preparations)
facsimile coins and bills such as Teaching Resources' *Coins
    and Bills*
optional: lined paper, 1 sheet for each child; and pens or
    pencils, 1 for each child

Advance Preparations

Either you or the children should cut out pictures of items
and their prices. Cut the construction paper sheets in half,
and tape or glue one item and its price to each six-inch by
nine-inch sheet.

Optional: Prepare a list of questions for the children to
answer, such as:

1. What is the price of the most expensive item?
2. What is the price of the least expensive item?
3. Does your item cost more or less than $5.00?
4. If you paid for your item with a $10 bill, how much
    change would you get back?
5. If you had a $20 bill, what items would you buy?

Directions

This activity may be done with an individual child or with
a small group. Each child looks at the items and chooses the
one he or she would like to buy. The child takes the sheet,
reads the price of the item, and then counts out that amount
of money in coins and bills and places the money on the
sheet. Write your questions on the chalkboard, or if you
are working with an individual child, give the child the list.
The child answers the questions either orally or in writing.

Individual Educational Objectives

Reading prices, making value comparisons, counting
money, and making change are skills fostered by this
activity.

**Big
Money
Mat**

Big Money Mat

Introduction

Activities with the Big Money Mat are an enjoyable way to provide supplementary learning experiences for children who are at the beginning level of money-skills development. The mat's large size and its tactile surface motivate the children's intellectual curiosity and encourage physical activity, which makes learning about money a pleasurable game activity. The mat activities in this section involve a variety of skills.

coin and bill recognition
value identification
counting skills
set and number concepts
matching skills
listening skills
sequencing skills
size discrimination
figure-ground discrimination
tactile-kinesthetic awareness
general body coordination
eye-hand coordination
perception of spatial relationships
language skills

The mat may be used with an individual child or with small groups of two to eight children. Larger groups also may be involved if you permit some children to watch while others are doing an activity and then rotate turns with them. The mat may be placed on a table or on the floor for the most effective learning situation. For some activities, it could be taped lengthwise on the wall. With the mat on the floor, the children can sit, kneel, or stand around the mat and walk or crawl on it or around it for various activities.

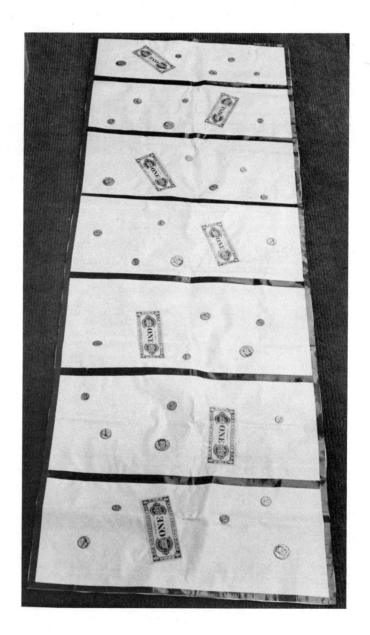

How to Make the Big Money Mat

Materials Needed

sheet of heavyweight plasticized cloth or oilcloth, white on at least one side, about 22" × 70"
roll of black tape, ½" to 1" wide and at least 154" long
white resin-based decoupage glue
facsimile coins and bills such as Teaching Resources' *Coins and Bills* — 7 pennies, nickels, dimes, quarters, half dollars, and one-dollar bills
optional: red tape for outlining border of mat

Directions

Outline the mat's border with black or red tape. With black tape, divide the mat into seven equal sections (10 inches each) as shown in the photograph. Put a one-dollar bill in each section so the bills form a series of "footprints" as you look down the length of the mat. Put a penny, nickel, dime, quarter, and half dollar in each section in a random arrangement but one that will allow a child to step easily from one penny (or other coin) to another along the mat's length. When you have arranged the coins and bills to your satisfaction, glue them to the mat. Use the glue liberally on the underside of each coin and bill, and then spread glue over the top surface of the coins and bills to decoupage them to the mat. This will prevent them from peeling off. Allow the glue to dry thoroughly before using the mat.

Gross-Motor Activities

Have a child stand at one end of the mat. Call out the name of a coin or the one-dollar bill. The child walks along the mat, stepping on that coin or the bill in each section. You also may want to have the child turn when he or she reaches the last section and retrace his or her steps back to the starting point. Have the other children watch and monitor for errors.

Instead of naming a coin or the bill yourself, you could have the children take turns being the "caller" and thinking of what to name. This helps them learn and remember the names of the coins and the bill.

You also could use a set of cards or a cube to determine the moves. The cards or cube could show names (*penny, nickel, dime, quarter, half dollar, one-dollar bill*), values in words (*one cent, five cents, ten cents, twenty-five cents, fifty cents, one dollar*), or values in numerals (1¢, 5¢, 10¢, 25¢, 50¢, $1). The teacher-made cubes from "Coin Cubes," page 42, or Teaching Resources' *Money Cubes* may be used. Each child in turn chooses a card or rolls a cube, reads what is shown, names the coin or bill, and then steps along the mat as described above.

Matching Activities

From one to seven children can participate in the following activities. Have the children sit (if the mat is on a table) or kneel (if it is on the floor) around the mat, spacing themselves so each child is in front of a section.

- Show a real one-dollar bill. Pass it around so each child can examine it and compare it with the facsimile bill in his or her section of the mat. Then give each child a real penny and have the child match it to the facsimile penny in his or her section of the mat, comparing size and features. Repeat this same procedure with the nickel, dime, quarter, and half dollar.

- Put a set of five real coins and a real one-dollar bill in a paper plate. Let each child in turn match the real coins and bill to the ones in his or her section of the mat and put them on top of the facsimiles.

- Put a set of five real coins and a real one-dollar bill in a paper plate. Let each child in turn choose one coin or the bill from the plate and then count the total number of bills or coins of that denomination on the mat. (The total is always seven.)

Elimination Game

This is a game for eight children. Have four children kneel (if the mat is on the floor) or sit (if it is on a table) on each side of the mat in a "ready" position with one hand poised at the edge of the mat. You or another child may be the "caller." The caller uses a cube or a set of cards with the names of the coins and the bill. The caller turns over a card or rolls the cube and then names the coin or bill shown. Instantly, each player covers that picture on the mat with his or her hand. This may require a child to get up and run around the mat to find and cover the correct picture. Since there are eight children playing but only seven pictures of each coin or the bill on the mat, one child will not be able to cover the correct picture. This child is eliminated.

Next, turn under or roll up one section of the mat so only six sections are showing. Repeat the "calling" and covering procedure. Again, there is one more player than there are sections showing, so one child will be eliminated. Continue this procedure until only two players and one section remain. This is the "play-off," and one child will be the winner.

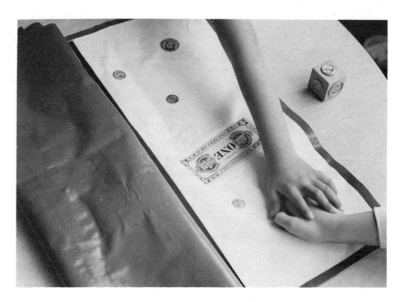

The mat has been folded up to the last section for the play-off. When the cube was rolled, David put his hand on the quarter first, so he is the winner.

If you wish to begin the game with fewer than eight children, simply fold or roll up the mat to eliminate extra sections. There should be one less section showing than there are children playing.

Variation: Two players can play the game like Slap Jack if the mat is folded or rolled up so only one section shows and the players use a cube or set of cards to determine the coin or bill they are to cover. The children could keep track of their scores by writing tally marks on paper or by taking chips, beans, or other counters from a draw pile.

Concentration Game

This game is played with an even number of sections showing on the mat. An even number is needed because a "match" in the game consists of two identical coin pictures. The bill pictures are not used. Fold or roll up the mat to expose only two, four, or six sections. The more sections used, the more difficult the game.

Cover each coin picture with a small card or paper square. (For a more orderly game, number each card or square and put it over the coin picture with the number side up.) One player at a time picks up any two cards and exposes the coin pictures underneath. If the coins match, the child takes the two cards. If they do not match, the child leaves them exposed long enough for the other players to see them and then covers them with the cards again. The next player then takes his or her turn. As coins are exposed and then recovered, the players try to remember the locations of matching pairs. After all of the coins have been matched, the player with the most cards is the winner.

Labeling Activities

From two to seven children may do these activities. Each child should position himself or herself next to one section of the mat.

- Print the words *penny, nickel, dime, quarter, half dollar,* and *one-dollar bill* on 2½-inch-square cards. Make seven sets, and use as many sets as there are children participating. Shuffle the cards and put them face down in a stack. Each child in turn draws a card, turns it over, reads the word, and then puts the card over that coin or bill in his or her section. If a child draws a card that he or she already drew in a previous turn, the card is put face down at the bottom of the stack. Continue until all coins and bills on the mat are covered.

- The same activity may be done using cards with the words *one cent, five cents, ten cents, twenty-five cents, fifty cents,* and *one dollar.*

- The activity also may be done using cards with the amounts 1¢, 5¢, 10¢, 25¢, 50¢, and $1.00 or $.01, $.05, $.10, $.25, $.50, and $1.00.

Collect the Money

This activity may be done with an individual child or with a small group of up to six children. You will need seven real or facsimile pennies, nickels, dimes, quarters, half dollars, and one-dollar bills. Put the coins and bills over the ones on the mat. You may want to have the children do this themselves as a preliminary matching activity.

Next, call on one child to respond to the following set of one direction and three questions. The child may answer the questions verbally, or he or she could answer the first two questions verbally and then all children could answer the last question in writing. (The response to the first question is always "seven.")

1. "Collect all the pennies on the mat." (The child should pick up the penny from each section and put them in front of himself or herself.)

2. "How many are there?" (Let the child count them out one by one if necessary.)

3. "How much is each penny worth?"(The child should answer "one cent.")

4. "How much are all the pennies together worth?" (The child could either calculate the answer mentally or count out the pennies again.)

Repeat the same direction and questions for each of the remaining coins and the one-dollar bill, and have a different child respond to each set. If the children are counting out the coins to find the answer to #4, they would count by fives for the nickels, by tens for the dimes, by 25's for the quarters, by 50's for the half dollars, and by ones for the one-dollar bills. The answers to #4 are: nickels, 35¢; dimes, 70¢; quarters, $1.75; half dollars, $3.50; and one-dollar bills, $7.00.

Variation: A different version of this game may be played using a cube or a set of cards with coin and bill pictures, names, values in words, or values in numerals. Each child in turn rolls the cube or draws a card and then identifies the coin or bill shown. The child then takes *one* example of that coin or bill from the mat and puts it in his or her collection. The game continues in this manner until all coins and bills have been collected from the mat. Each child then adds up his or her coins and bills to find the total amount of money he or she collected. The child with the most money is the winner.

Basic Shape Patterns for "Penny Rubbings in Patterns," page 44

Patterns for "Animal Banks," page 48

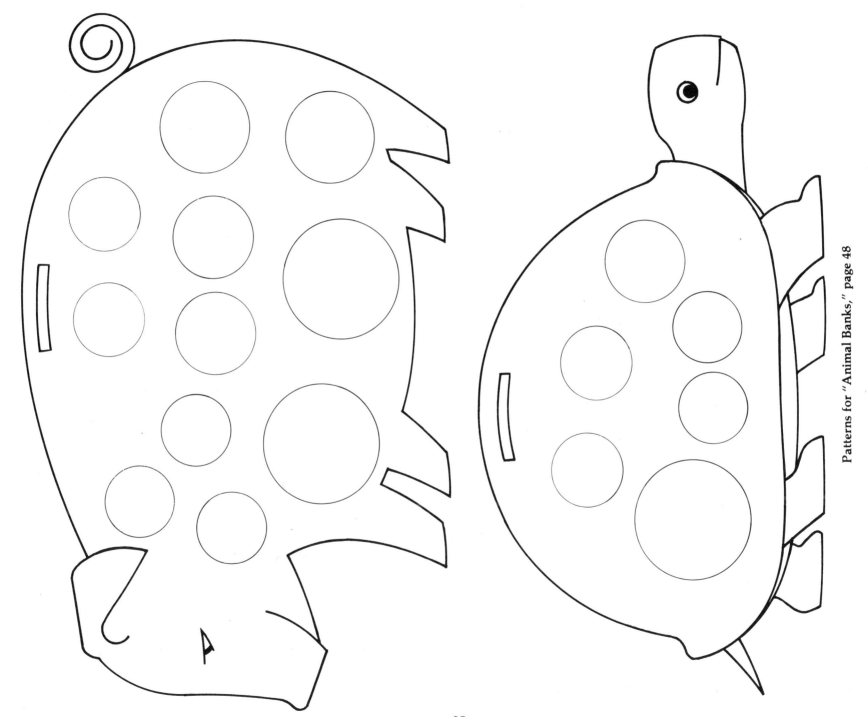

Patterns for "Animal Banks," page 48

85

Patterns for "Put Money in the Bank," page 49

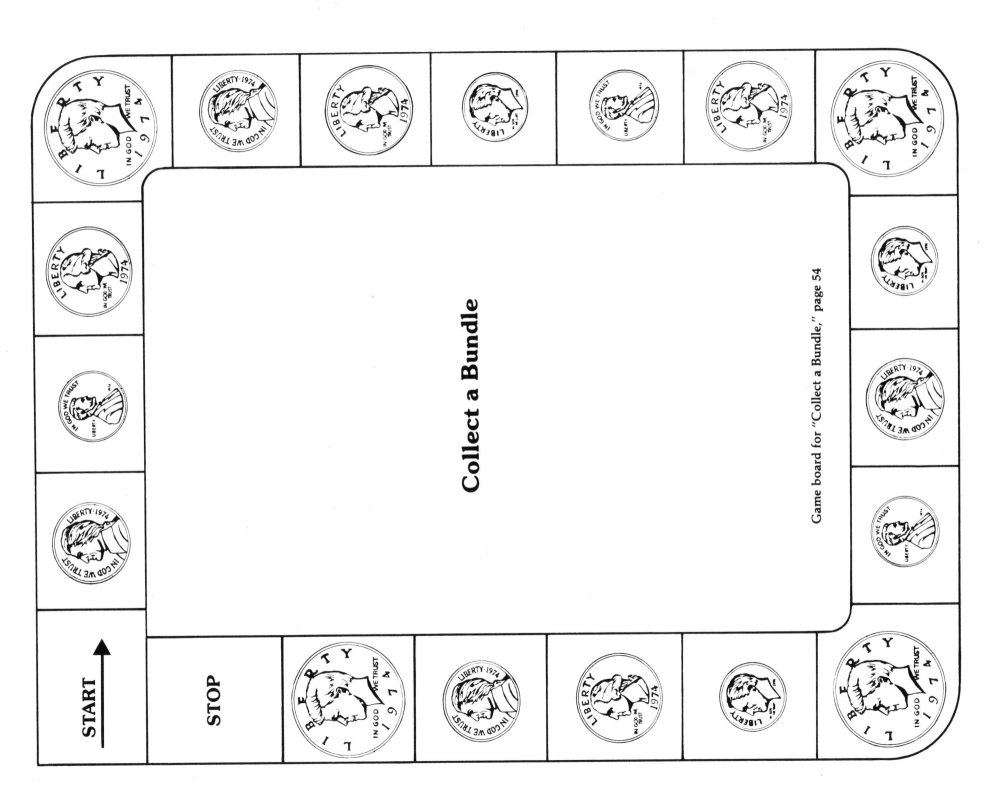

START

STOP

Collect a Bundle

Game board for "Collect a Bundle," page 54

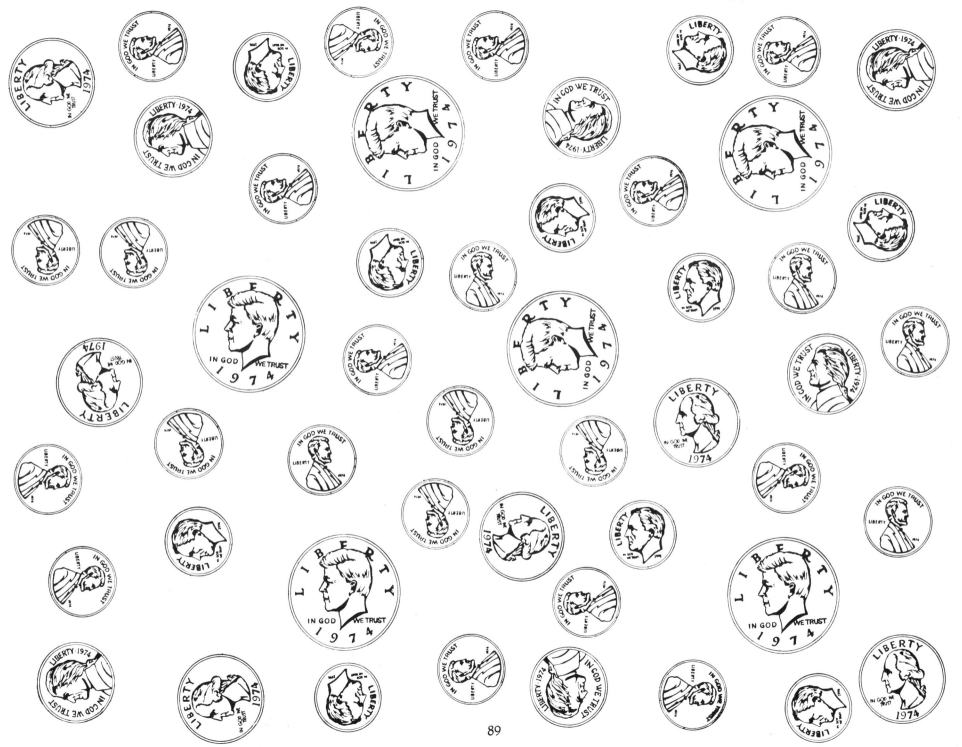

89

13. Point to the ten-cent coin.	1. Point to the half dollar.
14. Point to the five-cent coin.	2. Point to the quarter.
15. Point to the one-cent coin.	3. Point to the dime.
16. Which coin is worth the most amount of money?	4. Point to the nickel.
17. Which coin is worth the least amount of money?	5. Point to the penny.
18. Which coin is worth the same as two dimes and a nickel?	6. Point to the coin worth 50¢.
19. Which coin is worth the same as two quarters?	7. Point to the coin worth 25¢.
20. Which coin buys more than a quarter?	8. Point to the coin worth 10¢.
21. Which coin buys less than a nickel?	9. Point to the coin worth 5¢.
22. Which coins buy more than a nickel?	10. Point to the coin worth 1¢.
23. Which coins buy less than a dime?	11. Point to the fifty-cent coin.
24. Which coins buy more than a dime?	12. Point to the twenty-five-cent coin.

Instruction cards for "Point to the Coin," page 71